MUNICH TRAVEL GUIDE 2024

Your Complete City Pocket Manual to Discovering Top Attractions, Cultural Experiences, and Insider Tips for Exploring Bavaria's Heart with Maps, Pictures and Itineraries

Paul L. Lee

Disclaimer

We've carefully crafted the **Munich Travel Guide 2024** to offer you the latest and most comprehensive information about the city. However, keep in mind that details like *pricing, operating hours, and tour availability* can change. To ensure your visit goes smoothly, we strongly recommend verifying these details directly with *hotels, attractions, and other service providers* before your Munich adventure begins. While this guide serves as an essential resource for planning your trip, taking the extra step to confirm this information will help ensure your experience in Munich is truly memorable.

Table of Contents

Introduction

Munich has always felt like a second home to me. I've visited many times, but each trip feels like the first – it's a city that never stops surprising and delighting me.

In 2024, my visit was particularly special. It had been a while since my last trip, and I was so excited to be back. As soon as I landed, I could feel that familiar buzz of excitement. Munich was calling, and I was ready to answer.

My first stop was Marienplatz, the main square. The Glockenspiel clock is always a highlight – it's amazing to watch the little figures dance around and tell their stories. It's a tradition that never gets old.

Next, I headed to the Viktualienmarkt, the food market. It's a feast for the senses – colorful fruits and vegetables, beautiful flowers, and delicious smells everywhere. I couldn't resist trying some fresh strawberries and a warm pretzel.

The English Garden is a must-visit. It's like a huge park in the middle of the city. I love walking along the paths, seeing the Chinese Tower, and watching the swans on the lake. It's the perfect place to relax and enjoy nature.

As the sun started to set, I went to the Isar River. The view of the city is stunning, especially at dusk. It's so peaceful there – a great place to just sit and think.

The highlight of my trip was Oktoberfest. It's a giant party celebrating Bavarian culture. There are huge beer tents, fun rides, and everyone dresses up in traditional clothes. I had so much fun singing, dancing, and enjoying the festive atmosphere.

Leaving Munich was hard. I had made so many wonderful memories. But I know I'll be back soon. Munich has a special magic that keeps drawing me back.

If you're thinking about visiting Munich, do it! It's a city that has something for everyone – history, culture, beautiful scenery, and delicious food. You'll fall in love with it, just like I have.

Chapter 1: Discovering Munich in 2024

A. Welcome to Munich

Hey there, welcome to Munich! I'm thrilled you're here. You've made a fantastic choice picking this incredible city for your adventure. Whether it's your first time or you're a returning enthusiast, Munich has something special in store for you.

From the moment you step off the train or plane, you'll feel a certain magic in the air. The way the sun glints off the spires of the Frauenkirche, the crisp alpine breeze, and the friendly faces of the locals—it all feels like a warm Bavarian welcome. Munich isn't just another city; it's a place that embraces you with its history, culture, and Gemütlichkeit (a unique Bavarian sense of coziness and good cheer).

Your journey likely begins in the heart of the city, Marienplatz. Here, the grand architecture of the Neues Rathaus (New Town Hall) and the iconic Glockenspiel clock will leave you in awe. These buildings aren't just beautiful; they're living testaments to Munich's rich history. Wander through the charming streets, browse the shops, and grab a coffee at a traditional café. The locals are incredibly friendly and always up for a chat.

Munich is a wonderful blend of old and new. You'll hear the Bavarian dialect mixed with German and English, creating a unique cultural tapestry. And the food? Oh, the food! Munich is famous for its beer and pretzels, but there's so much more to discover. Imagine biting into a juicy Schweinsbraten (roast pork) with crispy crackling or savoring a warm Apfelstrudel (apple strudel). Every meal is a celebration of Bavarian flavors.

But Munich's charm extends beyond the city limits. Picture yourself hiking through the breathtaking Bavarian Alps, exploring the fairytale castles of Neuschwanstein and Hohenschwangau, or taking a day trip to the picturesque town of Salzburg. Whether you're seeking adventure or relaxation, Munich and its surroundings have it all.

What truly makes Munich unforgettable, though, are the people. The locals are fiercely proud of their city and its traditions. Whether you're clinking glasses at Oktoberfest or enjoying a quiet meal at a local tavern, you'll feel their genuine warmth and hospitality. In Munich, you're not just a tourist; you're a welcomed guest, and by the time you leave, you'll feel like part of the Munich family.

So, as you use this guide to plan your time here, remember to keep your heart and mind open. Munich isn't just a place to see; it's a place to feel, taste, and experience. Let the beauty, culture, and people of this city captivate you. Whether you're here for the beer, the history, or simply the Bavarian spirit, Munich is ready to give you memories that will last a lifetime. Welcome to Munich—your adventure begins now!

B. A Brief History of Munich

Munich, a city of captivating beauty and rich heritage nestled in the heart of Bavaria, Germany, boasts a history that stretches back over centuries, echoing the footsteps of emperors, artists, and innovators who have shaped its identity.

Early Beginnings:
The history of Munich begins in the 12th century when a settlement arose around a monastery established by Benedictine monks. The name "Munich" is derived from the Old High German word "Munichen," meaning "by the monks." In 1158, Duke Henry the Lion granted the settlement market rights, laying the foundation for its future growth and prosperity.

Rise of the Wittelsbach Dynasty:
In 1255, the Wittelsbach dynasty assumed control of Bavaria, and Munich became their seat of power. Over the centuries, the Wittelsbachs played a pivotal role in shaping the city's landscape and cultural development. They commissioned magnificent palaces, churches, and artistic endeavors, transforming Munich into a flourishing center of art and culture.

Cultural and Artistic Flourishing:

The Renaissance and Baroque periods witnessed a remarkable flowering of artistic expression in Munich. Renowned artists and architects, including the Asam brothers, left their indelible mark on the city's architectural treasures. The Residenz, a sprawling palace complex, stands as a testament to the Wittelsbach's patronage of the arts.

Challenges and Resilience:
Munich's history has not been without its challenges. The city endured wars, plagues, and political upheavals, yet it always managed to rise from the ashes, stronger and more vibrant than before. The devastation of World War II left scars on the cityscape, but Munich rebuilt itself, preserving its historical essence while embracing modernity.

Modern Munich:

Today, Munich is a thriving metropolis that seamlessly blends tradition with innovation. It is a global hub for technology, engineering, and automotive industries, attracting talent and investment from around the world. The city also remains a vibrant cultural center, hosting world-class museums, theaters, and festivals, including the world-famous Oktoberfest.

C. Munich Today

Modern Munich is a dynamic and cosmopolitan city that seamlessly blends its rich historical heritage with a forward-thinking spirit. It's a place where centuries-old traditions coexist harmoniously with cutting-edge technology and innovation.

Cultural Scene:
Munich's cultural calendar is brimming with events throughout the year. As of August 2024, you can still catch the tail end of the Tollwood Summer Festival, known for its eclectic mix of music, theater, and art. The Munich Opera Festival continues until the end of July, offering a feast for classical music lovers. And of course, the world-famous Oktoberfest kicks off in September,

promising a joyous celebration of Bavarian culture and camaraderie.

Technological Hub:
Munich has established itself as a leading center for technology and innovation. It's home to major companies like BMW, Siemens, and Allianz, as well as a thriving startup scene. The city's commitment to sustainability and green initiatives is evident in its numerous parks, bike-friendly infrastructure, and public transportation system.

Architectural Marvels:
Munich's skyline is a captivating blend of historic and modern architecture. The Frauenkirche, with its iconic twin domes, stands as a symbol of the city. The Residenz, a sprawling palace complex, offers a glimpse into the opulent lifestyle of the Bavarian monarchs. Meanwhile, contemporary structures like the Allianz Arena and the BMW Welt showcase Munich's innovative spirit.

Gastronomic Delights:
Munich's culinary scene is a treat for the senses. Traditional Bavarian fare like Schweinsbraten (roast pork), Weißwurst (veal sausage), and Brezen (pretzels) are readily available at cozy taverns and beer gardens. The Viktualienmarkt, a bustling food market, offers a cornucopia of fresh produce, cheeses, and delicacies from around the world.

Green Spaces:

Munich's commitment to preserving green spaces is evident in its numerous parks and gardens. The English Garden, one of the world's largest urban parks, offers a tranquil escape from the city's hustle and bustle. The Olympiapark, built for the 1972 Summer Olympics, is a popular destination for sports and recreation.

Beyond the City:
Munich's central location makes it an ideal base for exploring the surrounding region. Day trips to the picturesque Bavarian Alps, the fairytale castles of Neuschwanstein and Hohenschwangau, or the charming city of Salzburg are all within easy reach.

D. How to Use This Guide

This Munich Travel Guide 2024 is designed to be your ultimate companion for exploring the Bavarian capital. Whether you're a first-time visitor or a seasoned traveler, we've packed this guide with all the information you need to make the most of your trip.

Getting Started:

1. Welcome to Munich: Begin your journey with our warm welcome, where we introduce you to the city's unique charm and provide a brief overview of what to expect.

2. A Brief History of Munich: Delve into the city's rich past and discover how it evolved from a humble monastic settlement to a vibrant metropolis.

3. Munich Today: A Vibrant City: Get a glimpse of modern Munich, its cultural scene, technological advancements, and architectural marvels.

Planning Your Trip:

1. Before You Go: Find essential information on visas, currency, transportation options, and packing tips.

2. Getting Around: Navigate Munich with ease using our detailed guide on public transportation, taxis, and bike rentals.

3. Accommodation: Choose from a variety of options, from budget-friendly hostels to luxurious hotels, to suit your preferences and budget.

Exploring Munich:

1. Top Attractions: Discover Munich's must-see landmarks, including the Marienplatz, Frauenkirche, Nymphenburg Palace, and the Deutsches Museum.

2. Cultural Experiences: Immerse yourself in Bavarian culture at the Hofbräuhaus beer hall, the Bavarian State Opera, and the numerous museums and art galleries.

3. Day Trips: Venture beyond the city limits and explore the picturesque Bavarian countryside, fairytale castles, and charming towns.

Practical Information:

1. Dining: Savor the flavors of Bavaria with our recommendations for traditional restaurants, beer gardens, and cafes.

2. Shopping: Find unique souvenirs, traditional crafts, and high-end fashion at Munich's diverse shopping destinations.

3. Nightlife: Experience Munich's vibrant nightlife scene with our guide to bars, clubs, and live music venues.

Additional Features:

1. Exclusive Bonus: Authentic Traditional Munich Recipes: Bring the flavors of Bavaria into your home with our selection of delicious recipes.

2. Maps and Itineraries: Plan your days efficiently with our detailed maps and suggested itineraries.

3. Practical Tips: Get insider advice on everything from tipping etiquette to local customs.

Chapter 2: Getting to Munich

A. Arriving by Air: Munich Airport

SCAN THE QR CODE

1. Open your device camera app.
2. Position the QR code in the camera frame.
3. Hold your phone steady.
4. Wait for the code to be recognized.
5. Once recognized, tap on the notification or follow the prompt to access the content or action associated with the Qr code

As your plane begins its descent into Munich, you might catch glimpses of the Bavarian countryside, with its rolling green fields and distant Alps framing the horizon. This view is just a prelude to the seamless experience that awaits you at Munich Airport, officially known as Flughafen München. Located approximately 28 kilometers (about 17 miles) northeast of the city center, Munich Airport is not just a gateway to the city but also a microcosm of what makes Munich special: a blend of efficiency, warmth, and modernity.

Getting to Munich from the Airport

Munich Airport is incredibly well-connected, making your transition from the plane to the city center as smooth as possible. Once you land, you'll have a variety of transportation options to choose from:

1. S-Bahn (Suburban Train): The S-Bahn offers the most convenient and affordable way to reach Munich's city center. The S1 and S8 lines run directly from the airport to different parts of the city, with trains departing every 10 minutes. The journey takes about 40 minutes and costs approximately €13 for a single adult ticket. Tickets can be purchased at machines located in the airport or through the MVV (Munich's public transportation) website or app. This train service operates from early morning until late at night, making it easy to reach your destination regardless of when you arrive.

2. Taxis and Ride-Sharing: If you prefer a more direct route, taxis are readily available outside both terminals. A taxi ride to the city center typically takes around 30 to 40 minutes, depending on traffic, and costs between €60 and €80. Ride-sharing services like Uber are also available, offering a convenient alternative if you're looking for a more personalized service.

3. Car Rentals: For those who prefer to drive, Munich Airport hosts a variety of car rental companies, including Avis, Hertz, Sixt, and Europcar. The rental car center is located within the airport, and you can book a vehicle online ahead of your arrival to ensure availability. Renting a car offers the flexibility to explore Munich and the surrounding Bavarian countryside at your own pace.

4. Airport Shuttles and Buses: Several shuttle services and buses connect the airport to various parts of Munich and nearby regions. These services can be pre-booked online or arranged upon arrival. Prices vary depending on the destination and service provider, but they typically offer a good balance between convenience and cost.

Facilities and Services at Munich Airport

Munich Airport is more than just a transit point; it's a destination in itself. The airport boasts a wide range of amenities to make your arrival pleasant and stress-free:

- **Shopping and Dining:** From luxury boutiques to Bavarian delicacies, the airport's shopping and dining options are plentiful. Whether you're picking up last-minute essentials or enjoying a meal before heading into the city, you'll find something to suit your needs.

- **Wi-Fi and Connectivity:** Stay connected with free Wi-Fi available throughout the airport. This service is essential for navigating the city, staying in touch with loved ones, or simply passing the time.

- **Accommodation:** If you need to rest before heading into the city, consider staying at the Hilton Munich Airport, located directly between Terminal 1 and Terminal 2. This hotel offers luxurious rooms, a spa, and various dining options, all within easy reach of your arrival gate. For more budget-friendly options, nearby hotels like the Novotel Munich Airport provide shuttle services to and from the airport.

- **Visitor Information:** The airport's information desks are staffed by multilingual personnel who can assist with directions, bookings, and any questions you might have. Whether you need help navigating the S-Bahn or want advice on the best way to reach your hotel, the staff is there to make your journey as smooth as possible.

Visitor Park

Before you leave the airport, consider visiting the Munich Airport Visitor Park, located near Terminal 2. This park is a must-see for aviation enthusiasts, offering a viewing hill with panoramic views of the runways, historic aircraft on display, and interactive exhibits about aviation history. Admission is free, making it a great way to spend a few hours if you have time before heading into Munich.

Contact and Further Information

For more details on services, transportation, and amenities at Munich Airport, you can visit the official website: www.munich-airport.com. The website provides up-to-date information on flight schedules, booking options, and airport services.

Contacts:
- **General Inquiries:** +49 89 975-00
- **Car Rentals:** Contact individual providers such as Sixt, Hertz, or Avis through the airport's website or their respective websites.
- **Airport Shuttles:** Bookings can be made through the Munich Airport website or directly with service providers.

B. Train Travel to Munich

Traveling to Munich by train is a wonderful experience that offers comfort, convenience, and a glimpse of Germany's beautiful landscapes. Whether you're arriving from another German city or a neighboring country, Munich's Hauptbahnhof (Main Train Station) is your gateway to the city. Here's everything you need to know to make your train journey smooth and enjoyable.

Location and Overview of Munich Hauptbahnhof

Munich Hauptbahnhof is located in the Ludwigsvorstadt-Isarvorstadt district, just a short walk from Munich's city center. The station's address is Bayerstraße 10A, 80335 Munich, Germany. It's one of the largest and busiest train stations in Germany, handling over 450,000 passengers daily. This central location makes it a perfect starting point for your Munich adventure, whether you're heading to a hotel, a tourist attraction, or just exploring the city.

History of Munich Hauptbahnhof

Munich Hauptbahnhof has a rich history dating back to its opening in 1839, though the current structure was largely rebuilt after World War II. Over the years, it has evolved into a modern transportation hub while retaining its historical significance. The station has witnessed Munich's growth and transformation, standing as a symbol of the city's resilience and progress.

Types of Trains and Costs

1. Intercity Express (ICE): The ICE trains are the fastest and most comfortable option for long-distance travel within Germany. If you're coming from cities like Berlin, Frankfurt, or Hamburg, an ICE train will get you to Munich in the shortest time, often under four hours. Tickets can vary in price, typically ranging from €30 to €150 depending on the distance, time of booking, and class of service.

2. EuroCity (EC) and Intercity (IC): These trains connect Munich with other major cities in Germany and neighboring countries like Austria, Switzerland, and Italy. They are slightly slower than the ICE but still offer a comfortable and scenic journey. Prices for EC and IC trains range from €20 to €100.

3. Regional Trains (RE/RB): For shorter journeys within Bavaria or nearby regions, regional trains are an affordable and frequent option. Ticket prices for regional trains usually range from €10 to €30.

4. Night Trains (ÖBB Nightjet): For overnight trips, such as from Vienna or Rome, the Nightjet offers comfortable sleeping compartments, allowing you to arrive in Munich refreshed. Prices for a sleeper berth can range from €50 to €150 depending on the type of accommodation.

How to Book Your Train Travel

Booking your train tickets is easy and can be done in several ways:
- **Online:** The Deutsche Bahn website (www.bahn.com) and app are the most convenient options for booking. You can compare prices, select your preferred train, and reserve seats. The website is available in multiple languages, including English.
- **At the Station:** Tickets can also be purchased at ticket machines or service counters in the station. These machines accept major credit cards and cash, and they offer instructions in multiple languages.
- **Travel Agencies:** Some travel agencies also offer booking services, especially for international travelers who prefer a more personalized service.

Getting to Munich Hauptbahnhof

Munich Hauptbahnhof is easily accessible from all parts of the city and surrounding areas:

- **U-Bahn and S-Bahn:** The station is a major hub for Munich's U-Bahn (subway) and S-Bahn (suburban train) networks. Lines U1, U2, U4, U5, S1, S2, S3, S4, S6, S7, and S8 all serve the Hauptbahnhof, making it easy to connect from anywhere in the city.
- **Trams and Buses:** Several tram and bus lines also stop at or near the station, providing additional options for reaching your destination.
- **Taxis and Ride-Sharing:** Taxis are available directly outside the station's main entrances. A taxi ride within the city center usually costs between €10 and €20, depending on the distance.

Station Facilities and Services

Munich Hauptbahnhof offers a wide range of facilities to make your visit as comfortable as possible:

- **Shopping and Dining:** The station has numerous shops, including bookstores, fashion outlets, and convenience stores. Dining options range from quick snacks to sit-down restaurants offering local and international cuisine.
- **Luggage Services:** Lockers and luggage storage services are available, so you can explore the city without carrying your bags.
- **Wi-Fi:** Free Wi-Fi is available throughout the station, allowing you to stay connected while you travel.

- **Information Desks:** Multilingual staff at the information desks can assist with directions, train schedules, and other travel-related inquiries.
- **Opening Hours:** The station is open 24/7, but individual shops and services have varying hours, typically from 6:00 AM to 10:00 PM.

Contact Information

- **Munich Hauptbahnhof Address:** Bayerstraße 10A, 80335 Munich, Germany
- **Phone Number for General Inquiries:** +49 89 130810
- **Website for Deutsche Bahn (Booking and Information):** www.bahn.com
- **Luggage Services:** Available at the station; contact the service desk or check the station's website for details.

C. Driving to Munich

Major Routes to Munich

Munich is well-connected by a network of highways (Autobahnen) and roads that make driving to the city straightforward. Depending on where you're coming from, here are some of the main routes:

- **From the North (Berlin, Frankfurt):** If you're driving from Berlin, you'll likely take the A9 Autobahn, which leads directly into Munich. The journey from Berlin takes about 6 to 7 hours, depending on traffic and stops. From Frankfurt, the A3 Autobahn will take you to the A9, and the drive is about 4 to 5 hours.

- **From the West (Stuttgart, Zurich):** Driving from Stuttgart, you'll take the A8 Autobahn, which offers a direct route to Munich. The drive is approximately 2.5 to 3 hours. If you're coming from Zurich, Switzerland, you'll take the A96 Autobahn, which takes about 3.5 to 4 hours, depending on border checks and traffic.

- **From the South (Innsbruck, Salzburg):** For those coming from Austria, the A12 Autobahn connects Innsbruck to the German A8, leading into Munich. This scenic drive through the Alps takes about 2 hours. From Salzburg, the drive is even shorter, taking about 1.5 hours via the A8.

- **From the East (Vienna, Prague):** If you're driving from Vienna, the A1 Autobahn in Austria connects to the German A8, taking you into Munich in about 4 to 5 hours. From Prague, the journey is slightly longer, around 4.5 to 5.5 hours via the A93 and A9 Autobahns.

Tolls and Vignettes

Germany's Autobahnen are toll-free for passenger vehicles, but if you're driving through neighboring countries like Austria or Switzerland, you'll need to purchase a vignette (a toll sticker) before using their highways. Vignettes are available at gas stations near the border and must be displayed on your windshield.

- **Austria Vignette:** A 10-day vignette costs approximately €9.90 (2024 prices). It's required for driving on highways and is available at border crossings, gas stations, or online.

- **Switzerland Vignette:** A yearly vignette, valid from January to December, costs around CHF 40 (approximately €37). It's mandatory for all highways and can be purchased at the border or online.

Parking in Munich

Once you arrive in Munich, finding parking is something you'll need to plan for. The city has numerous parking options, but availability and cost can vary depending on your location:

- **Street Parking:** In central Munich, street parking is available but often limited. Most areas are metered, with prices ranging from €1 to €4 per hour. Pay attention to signs indicating parking zones and restrictions.

- **Parking Garages:** Munich has many public parking garages, particularly in the city center. Rates generally range from €2 to €4 per hour, with a daily maximum of €20 to €30. Some recommended garages include Park One Marienplatz and City Parkhaus am Stachus.

- **Park & Ride:** If you prefer to avoid the hassle of city-center parking, Munich's Park & Ride (P+R) facilities are an excellent option. Located on the outskirts, these facilities allow you to park your car and take the U-Bahn or S-Bahn into the city. Prices are very affordable, often around €1 per day, making it a cost-effective solution.

Driving in Munich

Driving in Munich is generally straightforward, but there are a few things to keep in mind:

- **Environmental Zones:** Munich has low-emission zones where only vehicles with a green emissions sticker (Umweltplakette) are allowed. These stickers can be purchased online or at certain inspection stations and cost around €5 to €10. Make sure your vehicle is compliant before entering these zones, or you could face fines.

- **Traffic:** Like any major city, Munich can experience heavy traffic, particularly during rush hours (7:00 AM to 9:00 AM and 4:00 PM to 7:00 PM). Plan your driving times accordingly to avoid delays.

- **Speed Limits:** On urban roads, the speed limit is generally 50 km/h (31 mph). On highways, speed limits vary, but in urban areas or near schools, the limit may drop to 30 km/h (19 mph). On the Autobahn, there's no general speed limit, but a recommended speed of 130 km/h (81 mph) is advised for safety.

Fueling Up

Gas stations (Tankstellen) are plentiful both on the highways and within Munich. Fuel prices can vary, but as of 2024, expect to pay around €1.70 to €1.90 per liter for gasoline and slightly less for diesel. Most stations accept major credit cards, but it's always good to have some cash on hand, especially at smaller stations.

Contact Information and Assistance

If you encounter any issues on the road, here are some important contacts:

- **German Emergency Services:** Dial 112 for emergencies (police, fire, medical).
- **ADAC (German Automobile Club):** For roadside assistance, contact ADAC at +49 89 22 22 22. They provide help with breakdowns, towing, and other vehicle-related issues.

D. Getting Around the City

Public Transportation: MVV (Munich Transport and Tariff Association)

Munich's public transportation system, operated by the MVV, is one of the best in Europe. It consists of U-Bahn (subway), S-Bahn (suburban trains), trams, and buses, all of which are integrated into a single network. This makes it easy to move around the city and even travel to surrounding areas.

- **U-Bahn (Subway):** The U-Bahn is the fastest way to get around Munich. It consists of 8 lines (U1 to U8) that cover most of the city and some suburban areas. Trains run every few minutes, especially during peak hours, and less frequently at night. The U-Bahn is ideal for getting to major attractions like Marienplatz, the English Garden, and the Olympic Park.

- **S-Bahn (Suburban Train):** The S-Bahn has 8 lines (S1 to S8) that extend further into the suburbs and surrounding regions. The S-Bahn is particularly useful if you're staying outside the city center or planning day trips to places like Dachau, Lake Starnberg, or even the Munich Airport. Trains run frequently, and the central hub for all S-Bahn lines is the Hauptbahnhof (Main Train Station).

- **Trams:** Munich's trams are a charming and scenic way to explore the city. The tram network covers much of the city center and some outlying districts, making it a great option for short trips or when you want to enjoy the view. Trams are especially useful for reaching places not directly accessible by the U-Bahn or S-Bahn, like certain neighborhoods or parks.

- **Buses:** The bus network complements the other forms of public transport, filling in the gaps where trains and trams don't go. Buses are reliable and cover almost every corner of the city, though they can be slower due to traffic. They are especially useful for reaching specific destinations like museums, parks, and residential areas.

Ticketing and Costs

Munich's public transportation operates on a zone system, with ticket prices depending on how many zones you travel through. Here's a quick overview:

- **Single Ticket:** For a short journey within one zone, a single ticket costs around €3.50. This ticket is valid for one journey, including transfers between U-Bahn, S-Bahn, trams, and buses.

- **Day Ticket (Tageskarte):** If you plan on using public transport multiple times in a day, a day ticket is your best bet. A single-day ticket for the inner city (Zone M) costs about €8.20, while a full network day ticket is around €13. This ticket allows unlimited travel on all forms of public transport for the entire day.

- **Group Day Ticket:** If you're traveling with family or friends, a group day ticket for up to 5 people is an economical choice. For the inner city, it costs around €15.60.

- **Weekly and Monthly Passes:** If you're staying in Munich for an extended period, consider purchasing a weekly or monthly pass. These offer substantial savings for frequent travelers and can be purchased at any MVV ticket machine or service center.

Tickets can be bought at machines located in every U-Bahn and S-Bahn station, as well as onboard trams and buses. The machines accept cash, credit cards, and debit cards. You can also purchase tickets through the MVV app, which is convenient and available in multiple languages.

Cycling in Munich

Munich is a bike-friendly city with an extensive network of cycling paths and dedicated bike lanes. Renting a bike is a great way to explore the city at your own pace, and it allows you to access areas that might be harder to reach by public transport.

- **Bike Rentals:** Numerous companies offer bike rentals across the city. Popular options include Call a Bike (operated by Deutsche Bahn) and MVG Rad (operated by the MVV). Rentals typically cost around €12 to €20 per day, with hourly rates also available for shorter rides.

- **Bike Tours:** If you prefer a guided experience, several companies offer bike tours of Munich, allowing you to see the city's highlights while learning about its history and culture. These tours usually cost between €25 and €35 and cover major attractions like the English Garden, Marienplatz, and the Isar River.

- **Safety and Etiquette:** Munich's cycling infrastructure is excellent, but it's important to follow local rules. Always stay in the designated bike lanes, signal your turns, and be mindful of pedestrians. Helmets are recommended but not mandatory.

Walking in Munich

One of the best ways to experience Munich is on foot. The city center is compact and walkable, with most major attractions located within a short distance of each other. Strolling through the streets of Munich allows you to soak in the atmosphere, discover hidden gems, and enjoy the city's beautiful architecture.

- **Walking Routes:** Popular walking routes include the stretch from Marienplatz to the Viktualienmarkt, a bustling food market, or a leisurely walk through the English Garden, one of the largest urban parks in the world. Walking tours are also available and are a great way to get acquainted with the city's history and culture.

- **Accessibility:** Munich is a generally accessible city, with most sidewalks and public spaces designed to accommodate people with disabilities. If you require assistance, many public transport stations offer elevators and ramps.

Taxis and Ride-Sharing

If you prefer door-to-door service, taxis and ride-sharing services like Uber are readily available throughout Munich. Taxis can be hailed on the street, found at taxi stands, or booked via phone or app. Fares start at around €4, with an additional charge per kilometer, so a short ride within the city center typically costs between €10 and €20.

Ride-sharing services offer a convenient alternative and often have slightly lower rates than traditional taxis. Both options are safe, reliable, and available 24/7.

Car Rentals and Driving in Munich

If you prefer to drive yourself, car rentals are available from various agencies throughout the city and at the airport. Major companies like Avis, Hertz, and Sixt have multiple locations. Renting a car allows you to explore beyond Munich, including day trips to nearby attractions like Neuschwanstein Castle or the Bavarian Alps.

- **Costs:** Rental rates vary depending on the car type and rental duration, but you can expect to pay between €40 and €100 per day, excluding fuel and insurance.

- **Parking:** Parking in Munich can be challenging, especially in the city center. Street parking is limited and metered, with rates around €1 to €4 per hour. Public parking garages are more reliable but can be expensive, with daily rates ranging from €20 to €30. Alternatively, Park & Ride facilities on the outskirts offer affordable parking with easy access to public transport.

Chapter 3: Where to Stay in Munich

A. Best Neighborhoods for Tourists

Altstadt-Lehel (Old Town)

If you want to be right in the center of everything, Altstadt-Lehel is the place to be. This is Munich's historic heart, where centuries-old buildings and modern amenities blend seamlessly. Picture yourself stepping out of your hotel and walking straight into Marienplatz, with its stunning New Town Hall and the famous Glockenspiel. From here, everything is within walking distance—beautiful churches like Frauenkirche, the bustling Viktualienmarkt, and plenty of museums.

Staying in Altstadt-Lehel means you're surrounded by history, and you'll never be far from a café to enjoy a Bavarian pretzel or a cold beer. It's perfect for first-time visitors who want to dive right into Munich's culture. Just keep in mind, because it's so central, accommodations here can be a bit pricier, but the experience is absolutely worth it.

Maxvorstadt

For the art lovers and history buffs, Maxvorstadt is your dream neighborhood. Known as the university district, it's full of energy, creativity, and youthful spirit. This area is home to some of Munich's best museums, including the Alte Pinakothek, Neue Pinakothek, and the Pinakothek der Moderne. Imagine spending your days exploring world-class art galleries and your evenings enjoying a meal at a cozy restaurant with a view of Ludwigstrasse.

Maxvorstadt is also close to the English Garden, one of the largest urban parks in the world. It's a great place to stay if you love walking or cycling in beautiful green spaces. The vibe here is a bit more relaxed than Altstadt, but you're still close enough to the center to easily visit all the main attractions.

Glockenbachviertel and Isarvorstadt

If you're looking for a neighborhood with a cool, modern feel, head to Glockenbachviertel. This area, along with nearby Isarvorstadt, is one of Munich's trendiest spots. It's known for its vibrant nightlife, stylish boutiques, and diverse dining options. Whether you're into hip bars, international cuisine, or unique shops, you'll find it here.

Glockenbachviertel is also the LGBTQ+ hub of Munich, known for its welcoming atmosphere and lively events. It's the perfect place if you want to experience Munich's contemporary side, with plenty of opportunities to meet locals and other travelers.

Schwabing

Schwabing is where Munich's bohemian spirit thrives. Once the home of artists and writers, this neighborhood still has a creative, laid-back vibe. Walking through Schwabing, you'll find leafy streets lined with cafés, boutiques, and art galleries. The area is also close to the University of Munich, giving it a youthful, intellectual energy.

Staying in Schwabing means you're near the English Garden, perfect for morning jogs or leisurely strolls. It's a great choice for those who want to stay in a lively, yet relaxed part of the city, with plenty of character and charm.

Haidhausen

If you prefer a quieter, more residential feel with easy access to the city center, Haidhausen might be the perfect spot. Located just across the river from Altstadt, this neighborhood has a village-like charm with its historic buildings and cozy cafés. It's a lovely area to stay in if you want to experience local life while still being close to all the major sights.

Haidhausen is also home to the Gasteig cultural center, where you can catch a concert or performance. And with its many beautiful squares, like Wiener Platz, it's a wonderful place for leisurely breakfasts and evening drinks.

Nymphenburg

For those who enjoy a more peaceful, suburban vibe with a touch of royalty, Nymphenburg is a fantastic choice. This neighborhood is home to the magnificent Nymphenburg Palace, a Baroque masterpiece surrounded by stunning gardens. Staying here gives you the feeling of being in a grand, historic setting, while still being just a short tram ride from the city center.

Nymphenburg is ideal if you're looking for a quiet retreat after a day of sightseeing. The area is also great for families, with plenty of green spaces and a relaxed atmosphere.

B. Luxury Accommodations

1. Hotel Bayerischer Hof

- **Location:** Promenadeplatz 2-6, 80333 Munich, Germany
- **Phone:** +49 89 2120 0
- **Website:** www.bayerischerhof.de

The Hotel Bayerischer Hof is not just a hotel; it's a landmark of luxury in Munich. Located right in the heart of the city, this five-star hotel has been welcoming guests since 1841. Over the years, it has hosted countless celebrities, royalty, and dignitaries, making it a part of Munich's history. Imagine stepping into a grand lobby where old-world charm meets modern elegance, and you'll understand why the Bayerischer Hof is so beloved.

The hotel offers a variety of rooms and suites, each designed with comfort and style in mind. The top-floor Blue Spa is a highlight, offering stunning views of Munich's skyline, a pool, saunas, and a range of wellness treatments. The hotel also boasts several restaurants, including the Michelin-starred Atelier, where you can enjoy gourmet dining in a sophisticated setting.

Rooms at the Bayerischer Hof start at around €400 per night, and suites can go well above €1,000, depending on the season and availability. You can book directly through their website or by calling their reservations team. This hotel is perfect for those who want to be close to major attractions like Marienplatz, the Opera House, and the Residenz Palace, while enjoying the highest level of luxury.

2. Mandarin Oriental, Munich

- **Location:** Neuturmstraße 1, 80331 Munich, Germany
- **Phone:** +49 89 290 980

- **Website:**
www.mandarinoriental.com/munich

Tucked away in a quiet street in Munich's historic Altstadt, the Mandarin Oriental offers a blend of Eastern tranquility and Western elegance. This luxurious five-star hotel is just steps away from the lively Marienplatz, yet it feels like a serene retreat from the city's hustle and bustle.

The Mandarin Oriental is known for its impeccable service and beautifully designed rooms that combine classic Bavarian elements with Asian-inspired decor. The rooftop terrace, with its panoramic views of the city and the Alps, is a perfect place to unwind with a cocktail or take a dip in the heated pool. The hotel's Matsuhisa Munich restaurant, created by world-renowned chef Nobu Matsuhisa, offers exquisite Japanese-Peruvian fusion cuisine that will leave you craving more.

Rooms here start at around €700 per night, with suites costing significantly more. It's a splurge, but the personalized service, attention to detail, and luxurious amenities make it worth every penny. Booking can be done online through their website, or you can call directly to tailor your stay to your exact preferences.

3. Hotel Vier Jahreszeiten Kempinski Munich

SCAN THE QR CODE

1. Open your device camera app.
2. Position the QR code in the camera frame.
3. Hold your phone steady.
4. Wait for the code to be recognized.
5. Once recognized, tap on the notification or follow the prompt to access the content or action associated with the Qr code

- **Location:** Maximilianstraße 17, 80539 Munich, Germany
- **Phone:** +49 89 2125 2799

- **Website:**
  www.kempinski.com/en/munich/hotel-vier-jahreszeiten

The Hotel Vier Jahreszeiten Kempinski is another jewel in Munich's luxury hotel crown. Situated on the prestigious Maximilianstraße, this hotel has been a symbol of elegance and sophistication since it opened in 1858. Staying here means you're in one of Munich's most fashionable districts, surrounded by high-end boutiques, theaters, and historical sites.

The hotel's interior is a blend of timeless elegance and modern comfort. Each room is uniquely decorated, offering a luxurious sanctuary after a day of exploring the city. The Kempinski's spa is a haven of relaxation, with a stunning indoor pool, a sauna, and a range of treatments to rejuvenate both body and mind.

Rooms at the Hotel Vier Jahreszeiten Kempinski start at approximately €450 per night, with suites offering even more luxury and space at higher rates. Reservations can be made through their website or by contacting their reservations team. This hotel is ideal for travelers who want to indulge in luxury while being close to Munich's best shopping and cultural experiences.

4. Sofitel Munich Bayerpost

SCAN THE QR CODE

1. Open your device camera app.
2. Position the QR code in the camera frame.
3. Hold your phone steady.
4. Wait for the code to be recognized.
5. Once recognized, tap on the notification or follow the prompt to access the content or action associated with the Qr code

- **Location:** Bayerstraße 12, 80335 Munich, Germany
- **Phone:** +49 89 599480
- **Website:** www.sofitel-munich.com

Housed in a stunning historic building that was once the Bavarian Royal Post Office, the Sofitel Munich Bayerpost is a perfect blend of historical grandeur and contemporary luxury. Located near Munich Hauptbahnhof, this five-star hotel is an excellent choice for those who value both convenience and elegance.

The Sofitel offers spacious rooms and suites that are beautifully designed with a modern aesthetic. The wellness area, with its indoor pool, sauna, and fitness center, provides the perfect spot to relax after a day of sightseeing. The hotel's Schwarz & Weiz restaurant offers a gourmet dining experience with a focus on local Bavarian ingredients.

Rooms at the Sofitel Munich Bayerpost start at around €300 per night, with suites offering even more luxury. It's a great option for travelers who want to be close to the main train station while enjoying the refined comfort of a luxury hotel. You can book directly on their website or by contacting the hotel.

C. Mid-Range Hotels

1. Hotel Torbräu

- **Location:** Tal 41, 80331 Munich, Germany
- **Phone:** +49 89 242340
- **Website:**
  www.torbraeu.de

If you're looking for a hotel that combines history with modern comforts, Hotel Torbräu is an excellent choice. Located in the heart of Munich, just a short walk from Marienplatz and the famous Viktualienmarkt, this family-run hotel has been welcoming guests since 1490, making it one of the oldest hotels in the city.

Hotel Torbräu offers cozy, well-appointed rooms with a classic European feel. The staff is known for their warm hospitality and personalized service, making you feel right at home. The hotel also features a delightful breakfast buffet that's perfect for starting your day.

Rooms at Hotel Torbräu typically range from €150 to €250 per night, depending on the season and room type. You can book directly through their website or by calling the hotel. This hotel is ideal for travelers who want to stay in a central location with easy access to Munich's top attractions, all while enjoying the charm of a historic hotel.

2. Motel One München-Sendlinger Tor

- **Location:** Herzog-Wilhelm-Straße 28, 80331 Munich, Germany
- **Phone:** +49 89 5177740

- **Website:**
  [www.motel-one.com](https://www.motel-o
  ne.com/en/hotels/munich/hotel-munich-send
  linger-tor)

Motel One is a popular choice for budget-conscious travelers who don't want to sacrifice style or convenience. The Motel One München-Sendlinger Tor is perfectly located near the historic Sendlinger Tor gate, placing you just minutes from Marienplatz and the shopping streets of the Altstadt.

The hotel features chic, modern rooms with a minimalist design, offering everything you need for a comfortable stay. Despite its budget-friendly rates, Motel One doesn't skimp on quality. The hotel's One Lounge serves as both a breakfast area and a bar, offering a relaxing space to unwind.

Room rates at Motel One München-Sendlinger Tor start at around €90 per night, making it an excellent value for its location and amenities. You can book through the Motel One website or by calling the hotel directly. This hotel is perfect for travelers who want a stylish, affordable place to stay in the heart of Munich.

3. Hotel Laimer Hof

- **Location:** Laimer Str. 40, 80639 Munich, Germany
- **Phone:** +49 89 1780380

- **Website:**
  www.laimerhof.de

For a more intimate, boutique experience, Hotel Laimer Hof offers a charming stay in the Nymphenburg district, just a short walk from the stunning Nymphenburg Palace. This family-owned hotel is housed in a beautiful 19th-century villa, providing a unique and personal touch to your Munich visit.

Hotel Laimer Hof's rooms are cozy and individually decorated, offering a warm and welcoming atmosphere. The hotel's owners are known for their exceptional service, going out of their way to make sure every guest has a memorable stay. The area around the hotel is peaceful and residential, giving you a quiet retreat after a day of sightseeing.

Rooms at Hotel Laimer Hof typically cost between €100 and €200 per night. Bookings can be made directly through the hotel's website or by contacting them by phone. This hotel is perfect for travelers who want to experience a more local, authentic side of Munich while still being within easy reach of the city center.

4. Hotel Metropol by Maier Privathotels

- **Location:** Mittererstraße 7, 80336 Munich, Germany
- **Phone:** +49 89 2444540

- **Website:**
  [www.hotelmetropol.de](https://www.hotel
  metropol.de)

Hotel Metropol is a stylish and comfortable hotel located just a short walk from Munich Hauptbahnhof, making it an ideal base for exploring the city. This modern hotel offers well-designed rooms with all the amenities you need for a pleasant stay, including free Wi-Fi, air conditioning, and a complimentary breakfast buffet.

The hotel's location is perfect for those who want easy access to public transportation, as well as major attractions like the Theresienwiese, home of the Oktoberfest. The surrounding area is bustling with restaurants, shops, and cafes, giving you plenty of options for dining and entertainment.

Rooms at Hotel Metropol start at around €120 per night, with higher rates during peak seasons like Oktoberfest. You can book directly through the hotel's website or by phone. This hotel is a great option for travelers who want a modern, comfortable stay with excellent access to Munich's transportation network.

5. Eurostars Book Hotel

- **Location:** Schwanthalerstraße 44, 80336 Munich, Germany
- **Phone:** +49 89 5999250

- **Website:**
  www.eurostarshotels.com

The Eurostars Book Hotel is a literary-themed hotel located in the vibrant Ludwigsvorstadt district, just a short walk from the Hauptbahnhof. Each floor of the hotel is dedicated to a different literary genre, with rooms and common areas inspired by famous books and authors. It's a unique and fun place to stay, especially for book lovers.

The hotel offers spacious, modern rooms with all the comforts you'd expect from a four-star property. The on-site restaurant and bar provide a convenient place to relax and enjoy a meal or a drink. The hotel's location is also perfect for exploring nearby attractions like the Deutsches Museum or the Oktoberfest grounds.

Room rates at the Eurostars Book Hotel typically range from €120 to €180 per night. Bookings can be made through the Eurostars website or by contacting the hotel directly. This hotel is ideal for travelers who want a bit of creative flair with their accommodations, along with a central location.

D. Budget-Friendly Options

1. Wombat's City Hostel Munich

- **Location:** Senefelderstraße 1, 80336 Munich, Germany
- **Phone:** +49 89 5998918 0

- **Website:**
  [www.wombats-hostels.com](https://www.wombats-hostels.com/munich/)

Wombat's City Hostel is a favorite among backpackers and budget travelers, and for good reason. Located just a short walk from Munich Hauptbahnhof (the main train station), this hostel offers a vibrant, social atmosphere and comfortable accommodations at a great price. Whether you're traveling solo or with friends, Wombat's is a fantastic place to meet fellow travelers.

The hostel features dormitory-style rooms with bunk beds, as well as private rooms for those who prefer a bit more privacy. All rooms are clean and secure, with lockers provided for your belongings. The hostel also offers a lively bar, a spacious common area, and a guest kitchen where you can prepare your own meals.

Dormitory beds at Wombat's start at around €30 per night, while private rooms can be booked for around €80 to €100 per night. You can make reservations through their website or by calling the hostel directly. Wombat's is an excellent choice if you're looking for affordable, social accommodations in a central location.

2. MEININGER Hotel Munich City Center

SCAN THE QR CODE

1. Open your device camera app.
2. Position the QR code in the camera frame.
3. Hold your phone steady.
4. Wait for the code to be recognized.
5. Once recognized, tap on the notification or follow the prompt to access the content or action associated with the Qr code

- **Location:** Landsberger Str. 20, 80339 Munich, Germany
- **Phone:** +49 89 54998080

- **Website:**
  www.meininger-hotels.com

MEININGER Hotel Munich City Center is another great option for budget-conscious travelers. Located near the famous Oktoberfest grounds at Theresienwiese, this hotel offers a range of accommodations, from dormitory beds to private rooms, making it ideal for both solo travelers and groups.

The hotel is known for its clean, modern rooms and friendly staff. Guests can enjoy a variety of amenities, including a guest kitchen, a game zone, and a bar where you can unwind after a day of sightseeing. The MEININGER Hotel also offers a daily breakfast buffet at an additional cost, providing a convenient and affordable way to start your day.

Dormitory beds at MEININGER Hotel start at around €25 per night, while private rooms are available for approximately €80 to €120 per night. Bookings can be made through their website or by contacting the hotel. This hotel is perfect for travelers who want to stay close to the action, particularly if you're visiting during Oktoberfest.

3. A&O München Hauptbahnhof

- **Location:** Bayerstraße 75, 80335 Munich, Germany
- **Phone:** +49 89 4523595800

- **Website:**
  [www.aohostels.com](https://www.aohostels
  .com/en/munich/munich-hauptbahnhof/)

A&O München Hauptbahnhof is a budget-friendly hotel and hostel hybrid located just a short walk from Munich's central train station. This property offers a range of room types, from shared dorms to private rooms, all at affordable prices. The location is unbeatable, making it easy to explore the city's main attractions.

The rooms at A&O München Hauptbahnhof are simple but clean and comfortable, with basic amenities to ensure a pleasant stay. The hotel features a 24-hour reception, a bar, and a lounge area where guests can relax. There's also a breakfast buffet available each morning, which is a great way to fuel up before heading out to explore Munich.

Dormitory beds here start at around €20 per night, while private rooms are available from €70 to €100 per night. You can book directly through the A&O website or by calling the hotel. This accommodation is ideal for travelers who prioritize location and affordability.

4. Hotel Uhland

Hotel Uhland

Hotel Uhland
Uhlandstraße 1, 80336 München, Germany

4.1 ★★★★☆

View larger map

Directions

Parkplatz

Dekanat der Medizinischen Fakultät...

ROSE Bikes München
Bicycle Shop

Uhlandstraße

Hotel Uhland

Lessingstraße

Blutspendedienst des Bayerischen Roten...

Café am Beethoven

Kirche Jesu Christi der Heiligen der Letzten Tage

Agentur 22 Werbe Google

Keyboard shortcuts   Map data ©2024 COWI, GeoBasis-DE/BKG (©2009), Google   Terms

SCAN THE QR CODE

1. Open your device camera app.

2. Position the QR code in the camera frame.

3. Hold your phone steady.

4. Wait for the code to be recognized.

5. Once recognized, tap on the notification or follow the prompt to access the content or action associated with the Qr code

- **Location:** Uhlandstraße 1, 80336 Munich, Germany
- **Phone:** +49 89 5433500
- **Website:** www.hotel-uhland.de

For those who prefer a more traditional hotel experience on a budget, Hotel Uhland offers charming, affordable accommodations in a quiet residential area near Theresienwiese. This family-run hotel is housed in a beautiful 19th-century building, giving it a cozy, welcoming atmosphere.

The rooms at Hotel Uhland are tastefully decorated and come with all the basic amenities you need for a comfortable stay. The hotel is known for its friendly service and peaceful setting, making it a great option for travelers who want to escape the hustle and bustle of the city center while still being close enough to explore all the major sights.

Rooms at Hotel Uhland typically range from €80 to €150 per night, depending on the season and room type. Reservations can be made directly through the hotel's website or by phone. This hotel is perfect for those who appreciate a quiet, relaxing environment with easy access to Munich's attractions.

5. Hotel Jedermann

- **Location:** Bayerstraße 95, 80335 Munich, Germany
- **Phone:** +49 89 543240
- **Website:** www.hotel-jedermann.de

Hotel Jedermann is a family-owned hotel that offers affordable, comfortable accommodations in a convenient location near the Hauptbahnhof and Theresienwiese. The hotel has a warm, welcoming atmosphere, with clean, well-maintained rooms and a friendly staff that's always ready to help.

Guests at Hotel Jedermann can enjoy a complimentary breakfast each morning, featuring a variety of options to suit different tastes. The hotel also has a cozy bar where you can unwind in the evening. Despite its budget-friendly rates, Hotel Jedermann provides a high level of service, making it a popular choice among travelers.

Rooms at Hotel Jedermann range from €70 to €130 per night, depending on the room type and time of year. You can book directly through the hotel's website or by calling their reservations team. This hotel is ideal for travelers who want a comfortable, affordable stay with easy access to public transportation and major attractions.

E. Unique Stays: Hostels and Boutique Hotels

1. Gspusi Bar Hostel

- **Location:** Oberanger 45, 80331 Munich, Germany

- **Phone:** +49 89 444895800
- **Website:**
  www.gspusi-hostel.de

Gspusi Bar Hostel is not your typical hostel. Located in the heart of Munich's Altstadt (Old Town), this stylish and modern hostel is perfect for travelers who want to stay somewhere with a bit of flair. The hostel combines a cool, contemporary design with a laid-back, friendly atmosphere, making it a popular choice for young travelers and those young at heart.

The rooms at Gspusi Bar Hostel are clean, comfortable, and thoughtfully designed, with a mix of dormitory beds and private rooms to suit different preferences. The real highlight, however, is the bar downstairs, where locals and travelers alike gather for drinks and conversation. The bar has a cozy, intimate feel, making it a great place to unwind after a day of exploring Munich.

Beds in the dormitory rooms start at around €30 per night, while private rooms are available for approximately €70 to €100 per night. You can book directly through their website or by calling the hostel. Gspusi Bar Hostel is ideal for those who want to be in the center of the action, with easy access to all of Munich's main attractions.

2. Hotel Louis

- **Location:** Viktualienmarkt 6, 80331 Munich, Germany
- **Phone:** +49 89 4111908 0

- **Website:**
  www.louis-hotel.com

Situated directly at the Viktualienmarkt, Munich's famous food market, Hotel Louis is a boutique hotel that exudes elegance and charm. This hotel is perfect for travelers who appreciate design and details, offering a unique blend of modern luxury and classic Bavarian touches. The location couldn't be better—step outside, and you're right in the middle of one of Munich's most vibrant areas.

Hotel Louis features beautifully designed rooms with high-quality materials, including handmade furnishings and luxurious linens. The hotel's rooftop terrace offers stunning views over the rooftops of Munich, making it a perfect spot for a morning coffee or an evening drink. The in-house restaurant, Emiko, serves contemporary Japanese cuisine in a chic setting.

Rooms at Hotel Louis typically start at around €200 per night, making it one of the more upscale boutique options in the city. Reservations can be made through the hotel's website or by phone. This hotel is perfect for travelers who want a stylish, luxurious stay in the heart of Munich's bustling market district.

3. Cocoon Sendlinger Tor

- **Location:** Lindwurmstraße 35, 80337 Munich, Germany
- **Phone:** +49 89 5999870

- **Website:**
www.cocoon-hotels.de

Cocoon Sendlinger Tor is a boutique hotel that brings a playful, retro vibe to your Munich stay. Located near the historic Sendlinger Tor, this hotel is just a short walk from the city center, making it a great base for exploring Munich. The Cocoon brand is known for its quirky, fun design, and this hotel is no exception.

The rooms at Cocoon Sendlinger Tor are compact but packed with character, featuring funky décor inspired by 1970s design. Despite the playful aesthetic, the hotel doesn't skimp on comfort, offering cozy beds, modern amenities, and plenty of thoughtful touches that make your stay enjoyable. The hotel also has a relaxing lounge area where guests can enjoy drinks and snacks.

Rooms at Cocoon Sendlinger Tor start at around €100 per night, making it an affordable option for those who want something a bit different. You can book through the hotel's website or by calling them directly. This hotel is perfect for travelers looking for a unique, budget-friendly stay with easy access to Munich's main attractions.

4. Jugend- und Familienhotel Augustin

- **Location:** Am Bavariapark 16, 80339 Munich, Germany
- **Phone:** +49 89 2114120

- **Website:**
  www.hotel-augustin.de

For travelers seeking a blend of history, design, and affordability, Jugend- und Familienhotel Augustin is a hidden gem in Munich. Located near the Theresienwiese, home of the Oktoberfest, this hotel is housed in a historic building that has been beautifully renovated to combine old-world charm with modern comforts.

The hotel offers a range of room types, including dormitory-style rooms for budget travelers, as well as family rooms and suites for those who want more space. Each room is uniquely decorated with a focus on sustainability and local craftsmanship. The hotel's communal areas are equally charming, with a lovely garden and a cozy lounge where guests can relax.

Dormitory beds at Jugend- und Familienhotel Augustin start at around €40 per night, while private rooms range from €100 to €150 per night. Reservations can be made through the hotel's website or by calling their reservations team. This hotel is perfect for families, groups, and solo travelers who want a unique and affordable stay with a touch of history.

5. Müller Inn Bed & Breakfast

- **Location:** Müllerstraße 43A, 80469 Munich, Germany
- **Phone:** +49 89 2602164
- **Website:** www.mueller-inn.de

If you're looking for a cozy, intimate stay in Munich, the Müller Inn Bed & Breakfast offers a charming alternative to larger hotels. This small, family-run B&B is located in the trendy Glockenbachviertel district, known for its vibrant nightlife, cool cafés, and eclectic shops. Staying here feels like being a guest in a local's home, with all the warmth and personal touches that come with it.

The Müller Inn offers a few beautifully decorated rooms, each with its own character. The B&B serves a delicious breakfast each morning, featuring organic and locally sourced ingredients. The hosts are known for their hospitality, providing guests with insider tips on the best places to visit in Munich.

Rooms at the Müller Inn start at around €90 per night, making it a great value for its central location and personalized service. Bookings can be made directly through their website or by phone. This B&B is ideal for travelers who prefer a more intimate, homely experience in one of Munich's most vibrant neighborhoods.

Chapter 4: Top Attractions in Munich

A. Marienplatz and the New Town Hall

Imagine standing in the heart of Munich, surrounded by centuries of history, culture, and vibrant city life. This is Marienplatz, the beating heart of Munich, and it's one of those places that you simply must visit when you're in the city. Whether you're here to explore the stunning architecture, soak in the local atmosphere, or just take in the beauty of this iconic square, Marienplatz and the New Town Hall are sure to leave a lasting impression.

A Brief History

Marienplatz has been the central square of Munich since the city was founded by Henry the Lion in 1158. It was originally a marketplace and the site for medieval jousting tournaments. The square is named after the Mariensäule, a Marian column erected in 1638 to celebrate the end of Swedish occupation during the Thirty Years' War. Today, Marienplatz is surrounded by historic buildings, including the New Town Hall (Neues Rathaus), which is the star attraction of the square.

The New Town Hall, a magnificent Gothic Revival building, was constructed between 1867 and 1908. Its intricate façade, adorned with statues and spires, is a masterpiece of architecture. The most famous feature of the New Town Hall is its Glockenspiel, a giant clock with mechanical figures that reenact historical Bavarian events twice a day. This charming performance draws crowds of tourists and locals alike, making it one of Munich's most beloved traditions.

Location and How to Get There

Marienplatz is located right in the center of Munich, making it easily accessible from anywhere in the city. If you're staying in the Altstadt (Old Town) or nearby neighborhoods, you can reach Marienplatz with a short walk. For those coming from further away, Munich's excellent public transportation system makes getting here a breeze.

- **By U-Bahn/S-Bahn:** Marienplatz is a major hub for Munich's U-Bahn (subway) and S-Bahn (suburban train) systems. Lines U3, U6, and multiple S-Bahn lines stop at Marienplatz, making it the most convenient way to reach the square.
- **By Bus/Tram:** Several bus and tram lines also stop near Marienplatz, including Tram

19, which offers a scenic route through the city.

- **By Foot:** If you're already in the city center, walking to Marienplatz is the best way to immerse yourself in the local atmosphere. The square is surrounded by pedestrian zones filled with shops, cafes, and historic sites.

What to Do at Marienplatz and the New Town Hall

Visiting Marienplatz isn't just about seeing the sights; it's about experiencing the energy and vibrancy of Munich itself. Here's what you can do while you're here:

- **Watch the Glockenspiel:** The Glockenspiel is one of the highlights of the New Town Hall. Every day at 11:00 AM and 12:00 PM (and at 5:00 PM during the summer), the clock's mechanical figures come to life, reenacting two stories from Munich's history. It's a must-see event that will transport you back in time.

- **Explore the New Town Hall:** Take a guided tour of the New Town Hall to learn about its history, architecture, and the workings of the Glockenspiel. The interior is just as impressive as the exterior, with grand halls and stunning staircases.

- **Visit the Tower:** For a breathtaking view of Munich, take the elevator to the top of the New Town Hall's tower. From here, you can see the city's skyline, including the nearby Frauenkirche and the distant Alps on a clear day. The tower is open daily from 10:00 AM to 7:00 PM, and the cost is approximately €4.

- **Shop and Dine:** Marienplatz is surrounded by some of the best shopping streets in Munich. From high-end boutiques to souvenir shops, you'll find plenty of places to browse. When you're ready for a break, head to one of the many cafes or restaurants around the square. Enjoy a traditional Bavarian meal or simply relax with a coffee and watch the world go by.

- **Attend a Festival:** Throughout the year, Marienplatz hosts various festivals and events, including the famous Christkindlmarkt (Christmas Market) in December. Visiting during one of these times adds an extra layer of magic to your experience.

Where to Stay and Eat Nearby

If you want to stay close to Marienplatz, you're in luck—there are several excellent hotels nearby that offer comfort and convenience.

- **Hotels:** The Louis Hotel is a boutique option located directly at Viktualienmarkt, just a stone's throw from Marienplatz. For something more classic, Hotel Torbräu offers historic charm and modern amenities, also within walking distance.
- **Restaurants:** For dining, consider visiting Ratskeller, located in the basement of the New Town Hall. It's a traditional Bavarian restaurant serving hearty dishes in a cozy setting. For something quicker, grab a bratwurst or a pretzel from one of the street vendors nearby.

Practical Information

- **Opening Hours:** Marienplatz is open 24/7, but the New Town Hall and its tower have specific visiting hours, generally from 10:00 AM to 7:00 PM.
- **Costs:** Visiting Marienplatz is free, but there are small fees for tours of the New Town Hall and access to the tower (around €4).
- **Best Time to Visit:** Marienplatz is lively year-round, but it's especially magical during the Christmas season when the Christkindlmarkt fills the square with festive lights, decorations, and stalls. For fewer crowds, consider visiting in the early morning or late evening.
- **Contact Information:** For more details, you can visit the official Munich tourism website

or contact the New Town Hall's visitor information at +49 89 23300.

B. Nymphenburg Palace

Step into a world of grandeur and elegance at Nymphenburg Palace, one of Munich's most magnificent attractions. This Baroque masterpiece, surrounded by lush gardens and tranquil waterways, offers a glimpse into the opulent lifestyle of Bavarian royalty. Whether you're a history buff, an art lover, or simply looking to experience the beauty of Munich, Nymphenburg Palace is a must-see destination that will transport you to a bygone era of splendor.

A Brief History

Nymphenburg Palace, or Schloss Nymphenburg, was commissioned in 1664 by Elector Ferdinand Maria and his wife, Henriette Adelaide of Savoy, to celebrate the birth of their long-awaited heir, Max Emanuel. Over the years, the palace was expanded and transformed into the grand estate we see today, with each generation adding its own touches of luxury and refinement. The palace served as the summer residence for the Bavarian rulers, offering them a retreat from the hustle and bustle of court life in the city.

The palace's stunning Baroque architecture is complemented by its beautifully landscaped gardens, designed by the famous French garden architect, Dominique Girard. As you stroll through the palace's rooms and grounds, you'll be transported back to an era of lavish banquets, elegant balls, and royal intrigue.

Location and How to Get There

Nymphenburg Palace is located about 6 kilometers (approximately 4 miles) northwest of Munich's city center, in the Nymphenburg district. Despite its suburban location, the palace is easily accessible by public transportation.

- **By Tram:** The easiest way to reach Nymphenburg Palace is by taking Tram 17, which stops directly in front of the palace at the "Schloss Nymphenburg" stop. The journey from the city center takes about 15 to 20 minutes.
- **By S-Bahn:** Alternatively, you can take the S-Bahn (suburban train) to the "Laim" station, followed by a short bus ride (Bus 51 or Bus 151) or a pleasant 20-minute walk to the palace.
- **By Car:** If you're driving, there is parking available near the palace, but spaces can fill

up quickly, especially during peak tourist seasons.

What to Do at Nymphenburg Palace

There's so much to explore at Nymphenburg Palace that you could easily spend an entire day here. Here are some of the highlights:

- **Tour the Palace:** Start your visit with a tour of the palace's main building, where you can admire the beautifully preserved state rooms and royal apartments. The Stone Hall, with its grand frescoed ceiling, is particularly breathtaking. Don't miss the Gallery of Beauties, a collection of portraits commissioned by King Ludwig I, featuring the most beautiful women of his time.

- **Visit the Museums:** Nymphenburg Palace is home to several fascinating museums. The Marstallmuseum (Museum of Carriages and Sleighs) showcases the elaborate carriages, sleighs, and riding equipment used by the Bavarian court. The Museum of Nymphenburg Porcelain highlights the exquisite porcelain produced by the Nymphenburg Manufactory, one of Europe's most prestigious porcelain makers.

- **Explore the Gardens:** The palace's expansive gardens are a masterpiece of landscape design. Take a leisurely stroll along the tree-lined avenues, relax by the ornamental lakes, and discover hidden pavilions and temples scattered throughout the grounds. The Amalienburg, a rococo hunting lodge within the gardens, is a true gem, with its delicate interiors and stunning Hall of Mirrors.

- **Boating on the Canal:** During the warmer months, you can rent a rowboat and paddle along the palace's central canal, taking in the serene beauty of the gardens from the water. It's a peaceful and romantic way to experience Nymphenburg's charm.

Where to Stay and Eat Nearby

While you won't find accommodations directly within the palace grounds, there are several excellent options nearby:

- **Hotels:** For a luxurious stay, consider the Hotel Laimer Hof, a charming boutique hotel located within walking distance of the palace. This family-run hotel offers personalized service and a cozy atmosphere, perfect for those who want to stay close to Nymphenburg.
- **Dining:** After exploring the palace, you can enjoy a meal at the Palmenhaus Café, located within the botanical gardens of Nymphenburg. The café offers a delightful selection of Bavarian and international

dishes, served in a beautiful greenhouse setting. For a more casual option, grab a snack or coffee at one of the nearby cafés.

Practical Information

- **Opening Hours:** Nymphenburg Palace is open daily from 9:00 AM to 6:00 PM during the summer months (April to October) and from 10:00 AM to 4:00 PM in the winter (November to March). The gardens are open year-round from sunrise to sunset.
- **Costs:** Admission to the palace, museums, and gardens is around €15 for adults. Combination tickets are available if you wish to visit multiple attractions within the palace grounds. Boating on the canal costs around €15 per hour.
- **Best Time to Visit:** The best time to visit Nymphenburg Palace is during the spring and summer months when the gardens are in full bloom. However, the palace's interior is equally impressive year-round, making it a worthwhile destination no matter when you visit.
- **Contact Information:** For more details, visit the official website at www.schloss-nymphenburg.de or contact the palace at +49 89 17908-0.

C. The English Garden

Welcome to the English Garden, one of Munich's most beloved and iconic attractions. Whether you're looking to unwind with a leisurely stroll, enjoy a picnic by the lake, or watch surfers ride the waves in the heart of the city, the English Garden offers something for everyone.

A Brief History

The English Garden, or Englischer Garten as it's known in German, is one of the largest urban parks in the world, even larger than New York's Central Park. It was created in 1789 by Sir Benjamin Thompson, later known as Count Rumford, an American-born British physicist who served the Bavarian government. The park was designed in the style of an English landscape garden, which was popular in Europe at the time, and was intended as a public park for the enjoyment of all Munich residents.

Over the centuries, the English Garden has evolved into a vibrant, multi-purpose space that reflects both the city's rich history and its love of outdoor activities. Today, it's a place where you can experience the beauty of nature, the charm of Bavarian traditions, and the energy of Munich's lively social scene—all in one incredible location.

Location and How to Get There

The English Garden stretches from the city center to the northeastern outskirts of Munich, making it easily accessible from many parts of the city. The park is bordered by the Isar River to the east and the neighborhoods of Schwabing and Lehel to the west.

- **By U-Bahn:** The nearest U-Bahn stations are Odeonsplatz (U3/U6) and Münchner Freiheit (U3/U6), both of which are within walking distance of the park's main entrances.
- **By Tram:** Tram 18 stops at Tivolistraße, close to the southern part of the park. For access to the northern part of the park, you can take Tram 16 to Tivolistraße or take the tram to Münchner Freiheit.
- **By Foot or Bike:** If you're staying in the city center or in the Schwabing district, walking or biking to the English Garden is a great way to start your visit. The park has extensive bike paths, and cycling is one of the most popular ways to explore its vast expanse.

What to Do in the English Garden

There's no shortage of activities to enjoy in the English Garden, whether you're looking to relax, get active, or simply take in the sights:

- **Watch the Surfers at the Eisbachwelle:** One of the most unique attractions in the English Garden is the Eisbachwelle, a man-made wave on the Eisbach River where surfers ride the waves year-round, even in winter. It's a must-see spectacle that draws crowds of onlookers and is a testament to Munich's love of outdoor sports.

- **Relax by the Kleinhesseloher See:** The Kleinhesseloher See is a picturesque lake located in the southern part of the park. You can rent a paddleboat to explore the lake, or simply relax on the grassy banks and enjoy the peaceful surroundings. There are also several beer gardens nearby where you can enjoy a refreshing drink or a traditional Bavarian meal.

- **Visit the Chinese Tower:** The Chinesischer Turm (Chinese Tower) is one of the park's most famous landmarks. This 25-meter-tall wooden pagoda was originally built in 1790 and is surrounded by one of Munich's largest beer gardens. On weekends, you can often hear live Bavarian music played by a traditional oompah band while you enjoy a cold beer and a pretzel.

- **Explore the Monopteros:** For panoramic views of the park and the Munich skyline, head to the Monopteros, a small Greek-style temple perched on a hill. It's a great spot for photos, especially at sunset.

- **Stroll Through the Meadows and Woodlands:** The English Garden offers miles of walking and cycling paths that wind through meadows, forests, and along the banks of the Isar River. It's the perfect place to escape the city's hustle and bustle and immerse yourself in nature.

Where to Stay and Eat Nearby

While there are no accommodations directly within the English Garden, the surrounding neighborhoods of Schwabing and Lehel offer plenty of options:

- **Hotels:** For a luxurious stay close to the park, consider the Hilton Munich Park, which is located right on the edge of the English Garden. This hotel offers modern amenities and beautiful views of the park. For a more boutique experience, Hotel La Maison in Schwabing offers stylish accommodations just a short walk from the park.

- **Dining:** The English Garden is home to several beer gardens where you can enjoy traditional Bavarian food and drink. The beer garden at the Chinese Tower is the largest, but the Seehaus beer garden, located by the Kleinhesseloher See, is another great option, offering a more tranquil setting by the water. If you're looking for something more upscale, the Käfer-Schänke restaurant, located near the southern end of the park, serves gourmet Bavarian and international cuisine.

Practical Information

- **Opening Hours:** The English Garden is open 24/7, and there's no admission fee to enter the park. The beer gardens and other facilities within the park have their own operating hours, typically from late morning to late evening.
- **Costs:** Visiting the English Garden is free, but you'll need to pay for activities like boat rentals (€5 to €15 per hour) or meals at the beer gardens (around €10 to €20 for a meal and a drink).
- **Best Time to Visit:** The best time to visit the English Garden is during the spring and summer months when the weather is warm, and the park is at its most vibrant. Autumn is also beautiful, with the changing leaves adding a splash of color to the landscape. Even in winter, the park has its charm, especially if you're brave enough to watch the surfers at the Eisbachwelle.

- **Contact Information:** While the English Garden itself doesn't have a central contact, the Munich Tourist Office can provide additional information about the park and its attractions. You can visit their website at www.muenchen.de or call +49 89 23396500.

D. BMW Museum and BMW Welt

For automobile enthusiasts, technology buffs, and anyone fascinated by innovative design, the BMW Museum and BMW Welt are absolute must-visit destinations in Munich. These iconic attractions offer an immersive experience into the world of BMW, showcasing the brand's history, its cutting-edge technology, and its vision for the future. Whether you're a lifelong fan of BMW or just curious about what makes this brand so legendary, a visit to these sites will leave you inspired and amazed.

A Brief History

The BMW Museum was opened in 1973, just across the road from the company's headquarters in Munich. It was established to celebrate the history and achievements of Bayerische Motoren Werke (BMW), which began as an aircraft engine manufacturer in 1916 before evolving into one of the world's leading automobile and motorcycle producers. The museum is housed in a striking, futuristic building often referred to as the "Bowl" due to its unique circular design.

BMW Welt, which means "BMW World" in German, is a more recent addition, having opened in 2007. It serves as both a showcase and a delivery center for BMW vehicles, and it's also a venue for exhibitions, events, and interactive experiences. Together, the BMW Museum and BMW Welt offer a comprehensive look at the brand's past, present, and future, making them a key destination for anyone interested in automotive excellence.

Location and How to Get There

The BMW Museum and BMW Welt are conveniently located in the northern part of Munich, near the Olympiapark. The two attractions are situated next to each other, making it easy to visit both in one trip.

- **By U-Bahn:** The easiest way to reach BMW Museum and BMW Welt is by taking the U-Bahn. Take the U3 line and get off at the Olympiazentrum station, which is just a short walk from both attractions.
- **By Bus:** Several bus lines, including the 173 and 180, also stop near the Olympiazentrum,

providing an alternative if you prefer to travel by bus.

- **By Car:** If you're driving, there is parking available at BMW Welt and nearby Olympiapark. However, public transportation is generally the most convenient option given Munich's traffic and parking conditions.

What to Do at BMW Museum and BMW Welt

Visiting the BMW Museum and BMW Welt is not just about looking at cars—it's about experiencing the innovation, design, and passion that define the BMW brand. Here's what you can do during your visit:

- **Explore the BMW Museum:** Start your journey at the BMW Museum, where you'll walk through a timeline of BMW's history. The museum features over 120 exhibits, including classic cars, motorcycles, engines, and concept vehicles. Highlights include the BMW 328 Roadster, the legendary BMW 507, and the BMW Isetta, a microcar that became an icon of the 1950s. The museum's sleek, modern design enhances the experience, making it as much an architectural marvel as it is a historical archive.

- **Visit BMW Welt:** After exploring the museum, head over to BMW Welt. This state-of-the-art facility is a showcase of BMW's current and future technologies. You can see the latest models up close, learn about the company's sustainable practices, and even test your driving skills in one of the interactive simulators. BMW Welt also offers guided tours, where you can learn more about the design and production processes that go into making a BMW.

- **Take a Factory Tour:** For a deeper dive into the world of BMW, consider booking a factory tour. These tours offer a behind-the-scenes look at how BMW vehicles are manufactured, from the initial design phase to the final assembly. You'll witness the precision and craftsmanship that goes into every car, and you might even get to see the production line in action. Factory tours are popular, so it's recommended to book in advance through the BMW Welt website.

- **Enjoy the Restaurants and Shops:** BMW Welt also features several dining options and shops. The Bavarian Restaurant Bavarie offers upscale dining with a focus on regional ingredients, while the Biker's Lodge provides a more casual atmosphere with views of the museum and Olympiapark. Don't forget to stop by the BMW Shop, where you can purchase exclusive BMW merchandise, from clothing to model cars.

Where to Stay and Eat Nearby

While there aren't hotels directly within BMW Welt or the BMW Museum, there are several excellent options nearby in the Olympiapark area:

- **Hotels:** The Leonardo Royal Hotel Munich is a stylish, modern hotel located just a short distance from the museum and BMW Welt. It offers comfortable rooms, a fitness center, and easy access to public transportation. Another great option is the Arthotel ANA im Olympiapark, which provides contemporary accommodations with fantastic views of the Olympic Park.

- **Dining:** In addition to the restaurants at BMW Welt, you can explore other dining options in the nearby Schwabing district. Tantris, one of Munich's most renowned fine dining restaurants, offers a Michelin-starred culinary experience just a few minutes' drive from BMW Welt. For something more casual, try Seehaus, located within the nearby English Garden, where you can enjoy traditional Bavarian dishes with a view of the lake.

Practical Information

- **Opening Hours:** The BMW Museum is open Tuesday to Sunday from 10:00 AM to 6:00 PM. BMW Welt is open daily from 7:30 AM to midnight, with specific exhibitions and tours available during regular business hours.
- **Costs:** Admission to the BMW Museum is around €10 for adults, with discounts available for students, seniors, and families. Entrance to BMW Welt is free, but some specific exhibitions and experiences may have a fee. Factory tours cost approximately €13 per person, and advance booking is required.
- **Best Time to Visit:** The BMW Museum and BMW Welt are popular attractions, so visiting during the weekdays or early in the morning can help you avoid crowds. The facilities are well-suited for all seasons, making them a great indoor option during the winter months.
- **Contact Information:** For more details or to book tours, visit the official website at www.bmw-welt.com or contact them at +49 89 125016001.

E. Munich Residenz

Imagine stepping into a palace that has witnessed over 500 years of Bavarian history, where each room tells a story of opulence, power, and artistic brilliance. Welcome to the Munich Residenz, the former royal palace of the Wittelsbach family, who ruled Bavaria for centuries. As the largest city palace in Germany, the Munich Residenz is a treasure trove of art, architecture, and history, offering visitors a chance to walk in the footsteps of kings and queens. Whether you're a history buff, an art lover, or simply looking to be dazzled by the beauty of the past, the Munich Residenz is a must-visit attraction.

A Brief History

The Munich Residenz began as a modest castle in 1385 and was gradually transformed over the centuries into the grand palace we see today. It served as the seat of government and the royal residence for the Wittelsbach dynasty, who ruled Bavaria from 1180 until the end of World War I. Each generation of rulers left their mark on the Residenz, expanding and renovating it to reflect the styles and tastes of their time.

The Residenz is a complex of buildings that includes ten courtyards and 130 rooms, with architecture ranging from Renaissance and Baroque to Rococo and Neoclassical. During World War II, the palace suffered significant damage, but extensive restoration efforts have brought it back to its former glory. Today, the Residenz stands as a testament to Bavaria's rich cultural heritage and its enduring royal legacy.

Location and How to Get There

The Munich Residenz is located in the heart of Munich, near the Marienplatz and Odeonsplatz, making it easily accessible from anywhere in the city.

- **By U-Bahn:** The closest U-Bahn station is Odeonsplatz, served by lines U3, U4, U5, and U6. From the station, it's just a short walk to the Residenz.
- **By Bus/Tram:** Several bus and tram lines stop near the Residenz, including Tram 19, which runs along the nearby Maximilianstraße.
- **By Foot:** If you're staying in or near the city center, walking to the Residenz is an excellent option, allowing you to take in the beautiful surroundings of Munich's historic core.

What to Do at the Munich Residenz

The Munich Residenz offers a wealth of experiences for visitors, from exploring its lavish interiors to admiring its impressive art collections. Here are some of the highlights:

- **Tour the State Rooms:** The State Rooms are the most opulent part of the Residenz, designed to impress visitors and demonstrate the wealth and power of the Wittelsbach rulers. Highlights include the Antiquarium, the largest Renaissance hall north of the Alps, and the Throne Room, with its grand chandeliers and richly decorated walls.

- **Visit the Treasury:** The Residenz Treasury houses one of the most significant collections of royal jewels, crowns, and ceremonial objects in Europe. Here, you can marvel at the intricate craftsmanship of these priceless artifacts, including the stunning Crown of Bavaria.

- **Explore the Cuvilliés Theatre:** This Rococo gem, located within the Residenz, is one of the most beautiful court theaters in Europe. The theater was originally built in the mid-18th century and has been meticulously restored to its original splendor. If you're lucky, you might even catch a performance here, as the theater is still in use today.

- **Stroll through the Court Garden (Hofgarten):** Adjacent to the Residenz is the Hofgarten, a peaceful Baroque garden perfect for a leisurely stroll. The garden features manicured lawns, fountains, and a central pavilion, making it a lovely spot to relax and take in the surroundings.

- **Admire the Artwork:** The Residenz is home to an extensive collection of paintings, sculptures, and decorative arts. The Residenz Museum showcases these treasures, offering a deep dive into the artistic achievements of Bavaria's past.

Where to Stay and Eat Nearby

The Munich Residenz is located in a prime area of the city, surrounded by excellent accommodation and dining options:

- **Hotels:** For luxury accommodations, consider staying at the Hotel Vier Jahreszeiten Kempinski, located just a short walk from the Residenz. This five-star hotel offers elegant rooms and top-notch service. If you prefer something more boutique, the Mandarin Oriental, Munich is another excellent choice, known for its stylish interiors and central location.

- **Dining:** For a taste of Bavarian cuisine, head to the nearby Schwarzreiter Tagesbar

& Restaurant, located on Maximilianstraße. This Michelin-starred restaurant offers a modern take on traditional Bavarian dishes. For a more casual experience, visit the Ratskeller, located in the basement of the New Town Hall at Marienplatz, where you can enjoy hearty Bavarian fare in a historic setting.

Practical Information

- **Opening Hours:** The Munich Residenz is open daily from 9:00 AM to 6:00 PM (April to October) and from 10:00 AM to 5:00 PM (November to March). The Treasury and Cuvilliés Theatre have similar hours, though they may vary slightly depending on the season.
- **Costs:** Admission to the Residenz Museum and Treasury is approximately €9 for adults, with discounts for students, seniors, and groups. A combination ticket that includes the Cuvilliés Theatre costs around €14. Children under 18 can enter for free. Tickets can be purchased online or at the entrance.
- **Best Time to Visit:** The Munich Residenz is a popular attraction, so visiting early in the morning or later in the afternoon can help you avoid the busiest times. The Residenz is particularly beautiful in the spring and summer when the Hofgarten is in full bloom, but it's a worthwhile visit year-round.

- **Contact Information:** For more information, visit the official website at www.residenz-muenchen.de or contact them at +49 89 290671.

F. Deutsches Museum

A Brief History

The Deutsches Museum, officially known as the Deutsches Museum von Meisterwerken der Naturwissenschaft und Technik, was founded in 1903 by Oskar von Miller, a visionary engineer with a passion for science and education. His goal was to create a museum that would make science accessible to everyone, not just academics. The museum opened its doors in 1925, and since then, it has grown to house over 100,000 objects, spanning various fields of science, engineering, and technology.

The museum's exhibits cover everything from the earliest human inventions to cutting-edge technology, offering visitors an in-depth look at the progress of science and its impact on our daily lives. With its interactive displays and hands-on exhibits, the Deutsches Museum is a place where learning is as exciting as it is informative.

Location and How to Get There

The Deutsches Museum is centrally located on Museuminsel, an island in the Isar River, making it easily accessible from all parts of Munich.

- **By U-Bahn:** The nearest U-Bahn stations are Fraunhoferstraße (U1, U2) and Isartor (S-Bahn lines), both of which are within a short walk from the museum.
- **By Tram:** Tram lines 16 and 18 stop near the museum at the Deutsches Museum stop.
- **By Foot:** If you're staying in the city center, it's an easy and scenic walk along the Isar River to reach the museum.

What to Do at the Deutsches Museum

The Deutsches Museum is vast, with more exhibits than you could possibly see in one day. To make the most of your visit, here are some of the must-see highlights:

- **Explore the Aircraft Exhibit:** One of the museum's most popular sections is its aviation hall, where you can see everything from early gliders to modern jet planes. The full-scale models, including the historic Junkers F13 and the Messerschmitt Bf 109, offer a fascinating look at the evolution of flight.

- **Visit the Mining Exhibit:** Descend into a realistic underground mining environment where you can explore tunnels and see how mining technology has developed over the centuries. This immersive exhibit is a favorite among visitors of all ages and gives a unique perspective on one of humanity's oldest industries.

- **Discover the Marine Navigation Section:** This section features a variety of ships, from ancient canoes to modern submarines. You can even step aboard a life-sized replica of a historic fishing boat or explore the inner workings of a submarine. It's a great way to understand the technology and innovation that have powered maritime exploration.

- **Interactive Science Exhibits:** The museum is filled with interactive exhibits that make learning fun. Try your hand at operating a steam engine, generate electricity using a dynamo, or explore the principles of physics through hands-on experiments. These exhibits are designed to engage both children and adults, making science accessible and exciting.

- **Planetarium and Observatory:** The Deutsches Museum also houses a planetarium and an observatory, where you can explore the wonders of the universe. The planetarium offers daily shows that take you on a journey through the stars, while the observatory provides the opportunity to view celestial bodies through a telescope. It's a fantastic experience for anyone interested in astronomy.

Where to Stay and Eat Nearby

While the Deutsches Museum doesn't have accommodations on-site, there are several great options nearby:

- **Hotels:** For a comfortable stay close to the museum, consider Hotel Torbräu, one of Munich's oldest hotels, located near Isartor. This historic hotel offers modern amenities and a convenient location within walking distance of the museum. Another excellent choice is Hotel Concorde, a boutique hotel in the heart of the city, offering stylish rooms and easy access to many of Munich's top attractions.

- **Dining:** After a day of exploring the Deutsches Museum, you might want to enjoy a meal at one of the nearby restaurants. Wirtshaus im Fraunhofer, a traditional Bavarian pub, offers hearty German cuisine and a cozy atmosphere. For something lighter, Münchner Suppenküche near Viktualienmarkt serves delicious soups and light fare made from fresh, local ingredients.

Practical Information

- **Opening Hours:** The Deutsches Museum is open daily from 9:00 AM to 5:00 PM. The planetarium and observatory have specific showtimes, which you can check on the museum's website.
- **Costs:** Admission to the museum is approximately €14 for adults, with discounted tickets available for students, seniors, and families. Children under 6 can enter for free. There is an additional fee for planetarium shows, typically around €5. Tickets can be purchased online or at the museum's entrance.
- **Best Time to Visit:** The Deutsches Museum can get busy, especially during weekends and school holidays. To avoid the crowds, consider visiting on a weekday morning. The museum is well-suited for visits year-round, but it's an especially good option on rainy days when you're looking for indoor activities.
- **Contact Information:** For more details, visit the official website at www.deutsches-museum.de or contact the museum at +49 89 21791.

G. Olympiapark and Olympic Tower

A Brief History

Olympiapark was created for the 1972 Summer Olympics, which marked a significant moment in Munich's history. The park was designed to reflect a new, forward-looking Germany, symbolizing peace, transparency, and openness. The architecture of the park, particularly the sweeping, tent-like structures of the Olympic Stadium and the transparent roofs, became an iconic representation of this vision.

Despite the tragic events of the Munich Massacre during the Games, Olympiapark remains a place of inspiration and resilience. Today, the park continues to be a vital part of Munich's cultural and recreational life, hosting a variety of events, concerts, and sports competitions, while also serving as a popular destination for tourists and locals alike.

Location and How to Get There

Olympiapark is located in the northern part of Munich, easily accessible by public transportation and car.

- **By U-Bahn:** The nearest U-Bahn station is Olympiazentrum (U3 line), which is just a short walk from the main attractions in Olympiapark.
- **By Tram:** Tram lines 20 and 21 also serve the area, with stops near the park.
- **By Bus:** Several bus lines, including 173 and 180, stop at or near Olympiapark.
- **By Car:** If you're driving, there is ample parking available at Olympiapark, though it can get crowded during major events.

What to Do at Olympiapark

Olympiapark offers a diverse range of activities and attractions that cater to all interests, from sports enthusiasts to history buffs and nature lovers. Here are some of the highlights:

- **Visit the Olympic Stadium:** The Olympic Stadium is one of the most iconic structures in Olympiapark, known for its revolutionary design and sweeping glass roof. You can take a guided tour of the stadium to learn about its history, architecture, and the 1972 Olympics. The tour also offers behind-the-scenes access to areas normally closed to the public, such as the athletes' locker rooms and the VIP sections.

- **Climb the Olympic Tower:** For the best views in Munich, head to the Olympic

Tower (Olympiaturm). Standing at 291 meters (955 feet), it's one of the tallest structures in the city. Take the elevator to the observation deck, where you can enjoy panoramic views of Munich and, on clear days, even see the Alps in the distance. The tower also houses a revolving restaurant, offering a unique dining experience with breathtaking views.

- **Explore the Olympic Village:** The Olympic Village, where athletes stayed during the 1972 Games, is now a residential area, but it's still worth exploring. The nearby Olympic Village memorial honors the victims of the 1972 Munich Massacre and provides a place for reflection.

- **Visit the Olympic Park Lake:** The park's central lake is a great spot for relaxation or a leisurely boat ride. You can rent paddle boats or simply enjoy a walk around the lake, taking in the serene surroundings.

- **Attend a Concert or Event:** Olympiapark is a major venue for concerts, festivals, and sporting events throughout the year. From open-air music festivals to athletic competitions, there's always something happening. Check the park's official website for the latest event schedule.

- **Explore the BMW Welt and Museum:** Located adjacent to Olympiapark, the BMW Welt and Museum offer a fascinating look at the history, technology, and future of BMW. It's a must-visit for car enthusiasts and those interested in innovative design.

Where to Stay and Eat Nearby

While there are no accommodations directly within Olympiapark, there are several excellent options nearby:

- **Hotels:** The Leonardo Royal Hotel Munich is a modern hotel located close to Olympiapark, offering comfortable rooms and easy access to the park's attractions. Another option is the Hotel Vitalis by Amedia, which is a short walk from Olympiapark and provides a relaxed atmosphere with all the necessary amenities.

- **Dining:** If you're looking for a place to eat within the park, the Olympia Alm is a popular beer garden located on a hill with great views of the park. It's a great spot to enjoy traditional Bavarian food and a cold beer. For a more upscale dining experience, visit the revolving restaurant in the Olympic Tower, where you can enjoy gourmet cuisine while taking in panoramic views of Munich.

Practical Information

- **Opening Hours:** Olympiapark is open 24/7, but individual attractions such as the Olympic Tower, Stadium, and museums have specific opening hours, usually from 9:00 AM to 6:00 PM. Check the park's website for details on specific attractions.
- **Costs:** Entrance to the park is free, but some attractions like the Olympic Tower (€9 for adults) and guided tours of the Olympic Stadium (€10 for adults) have admission fees. Tickets for events and concerts vary depending on the event.
- **Best Time to Visit:** Olympiapark is a year-round destination, but the best time to visit is during the spring and summer months when the weather is warm and the park is at its most vibrant. If you're interested in attending a concert or event, check the schedule in advance to plan your visit accordingly.
- **Contact Information:** For more information, visit the official website at www.olympiapark.de or contact the park at +49 89 30670.

Chapter 5: Munich Itinerary Planning

A. 3-Day Classic Munich Itinerary

Day 1: Exploring the Heart of Munich

Morning: Marienplatz and the Old Town

Start your Munich adventure in the heart of the city at Marienplatz, the central square that has been the city's focal point since its founding. Arrive early to watch the famous Glockenspiel in the New Town Hall, which performs at 11:00 AM (and again at noon and 5:00 PM in summer). Afterward, take some time to explore the stunning architecture of the Old Town, including the Frauenkirche, Munich's iconic twin-towered cathedral.

From Marienplatz, wander through the nearby Viktualienmarkt, a lively outdoor market where you can grab a coffee, a freshly baked pretzel, or even a traditional Bavarian sausage. The market is a great place to soak in the local atmosphere and sample some of Munich's culinary delights.

Afternoon: Munich Residenz and Hofgarten

After lunch, head to the Munich Residenz, the former royal palace of the Bavarian monarchs. Spend a few hours exploring the opulent state rooms, the Residenz Museum, and the Treasury, where you'll find a dazzling collection of jewels and artifacts. Don't miss the beautiful Hofgarten, a serene garden adjacent to the Residenz, perfect for a peaceful stroll or a short rest.

Evening: Traditional Bavarian Dinner

As evening approaches, make your way to one of Munich's famous beer halls, such as the Hofbräuhaus, for a traditional Bavarian dinner. Enjoy hearty dishes like schnitzel or pork knuckle, accompanied by a stein of local beer. The lively atmosphere, complete with live Bavarian music, is the perfect way to end your first day in Munich.

Day 2: Art, Culture, and Gardens

Morning: The English Garden

Begin your second day with a visit to the English Garden, one of the largest urban parks in the world. Rent a bike or simply stroll through the park's picturesque landscapes. Make sure to stop by the

Chinese Tower, where you can enjoy a morning coffee or a Bavarian breakfast in the beer garden.

If you're visiting during the warmer months, don't miss the Eisbachwelle, where you can watch surfers ride the man-made wave in the middle of the park—a unique and unexpected sight in Munich!

Afternoon: Museum Quarter (Kunstareal)

Dedicate your afternoon to exploring Munich's Museum Quarter, known as the Kunstareal. Here, you'll find some of Germany's most important art museums, including the Alte Pinakothek, Neue Pinakothek, and the Pinakothek der Moderne. Depending on your interests, you can choose to focus on one museum or explore several. Art lovers could easily spend an entire day here, but even a few hours will give you a rich cultural experience.

Evening: Dinner in Schwabing

In the evening, head to the bohemian district of Schwabing, known for its artistic heritage and lively atmosphere. Enjoy dinner at one of the neighborhood's many restaurants, where you'll find everything from traditional Bavarian cuisine to international fare. After dinner, take a leisurely stroll along Leopoldstraße, a bustling street lined with cafés, bars, and shops.

Day 3: History and Innovation

Morning: Nymphenburg Palace

Start your final day in Munich with a visit to Nymphenburg Palace, the grand Baroque palace that was once the summer residence of the Bavarian kings. Explore the opulent state rooms, the stunning gardens, and the various pavilions scattered throughout the grounds. The Amalienburg, a rococo hunting lodge within the palace park, is particularly worth visiting for its intricate interior design.

Afternoon: BMW Museum and BMW Welt

In the afternoon, dive into the world of innovation at the BMW Museum and BMW Welt. Located near Olympiapark, these attractions offer a fascinating look at the history, technology, and future of one of the world's most iconic automobile brands. The BMW Museum showcases the evolution of BMW's vehicles, from classic cars to futuristic concepts, while BMW Welt offers interactive exhibits and the opportunity to see the latest BMW models up close.

Evening: Olympiapark and Olympic Tower

End your Munich adventure with a visit to Olympiapark, the site of the 1972 Summer Olympics. Take a walk around the park, explore the Olympic Stadium, and if you're feeling adventurous, climb to the top of the Olympic Tower. From the observation deck, you'll enjoy panoramic views of Munich and, on clear days, even the Alps in the distance. For a final treat, dine at the revolving restaurant in the tower, where you can savor gourmet cuisine while watching the city's lights twinkle below.

Tips for Your 3-Day Visit

- **Getting Around:** Munich's public transportation system is efficient and easy to use. Consider purchasing a Munich CityTourCard, which offers unlimited travel on public transport and discounts on many attractions.
- **Timing:** Arrive early at popular attractions like Marienplatz and the Munich Residenz to avoid crowds, especially during peak tourist season.
- **Weather:** Munich's weather can be unpredictable, so pack an umbrella and wear comfortable shoes for walking. If visiting in winter, dress warmly and consider indoor activities like museums.

B. 5-Day In-Depth Munich Itinerary

Day 1: Classic Munich Sights

Morning: Marienplatz and the Old Town

Begin your journey at Marienplatz, the heart of Munich. Watch the Glockenspiel in the New Town Hall, which brings history to life with its mechanical figures. Afterward, explore the Old Town, visiting landmarks like the Frauenkirche, with its distinctive twin towers, and the nearby St. Peter's Church, where you can climb the tower for panoramic views of the city.

Afternoon: Viktualienmarkt and the Munich Residenz

After lunch at Viktualienmarkt, Munich's famous food market, head to the Munich Residenz, the former royal palace of the Bavarian monarchs. Spend the afternoon exploring the opulent state rooms, the Treasury, and the stunning Hofgarten, a peaceful garden adjacent to the palace.

Evening: Traditional Bavarian Dinner

End your day with a hearty Bavarian meal at one of Munich's historic beer halls, such as the Hofbräuhaus or Augustiner Bräustuben. Enjoy classic dishes like schnitzel or roast pork, accompanied by a stein of locally brewed beer.

Day 2: Art, Culture, and Gardens

Morning: The English Garden

Start your second day with a visit to the English Garden, one of the largest urban parks in the world. Stroll through the park's beautiful landscapes, visit the Chinese Tower, and watch surfers ride the Eisbachwelle, a man-made wave in the park's river. If you're visiting in summer, consider renting a paddleboat on the Kleinhesseloher See.

Afternoon: Kunstareal (Museum Quarter)

Dedicate your afternoon to exploring the Kunstareal, Munich's Museum Quarter. Choose from world-renowned museums like the Alte Pinakothek (Old Masters), the Neue Pinakothek (19th-century art), and the Pinakothek der Moderne (modern art and design). If you're particularly interested in classical art, the Alte Pinakothek's collection is a must-see.

Evening: Schwabing District

In the evening, head to the Schwabing district, known for its lively atmosphere and artistic heritage. Enjoy dinner at a local restaurant and explore the area's vibrant nightlife, with plenty of bars and cafes along Leopoldstraße and around Münchner Freiheit.

Day 3: Nymphenburg Palace and Olympiapark

Morning: Nymphenburg Palace

Spend your morning exploring Nymphenburg Palace, the grand Baroque residence of the Bavarian royal family. Wander through the palace's opulent rooms, admire the beautiful gardens, and visit the various pavilions, including the Amalienburg hunting lodge.

Afternoon: Olympiapark and BMW Museum

In the afternoon, visit Olympiapark, the site of the 1972 Summer Olympics. Explore the Olympic Stadium, take in the views from the Olympic Tower, and walk around the park's scenic grounds. Then, head to the nearby BMW Museum and BMW Welt to immerse yourself in the history and future of one of the world's most iconic automobile brands.

Evening: Dinner at Olympiapark

End your day with dinner at the revolving restaurant in the Olympic Tower, where you can enjoy gourmet cuisine while taking in panoramic views of Munich.

Day 4: Day Trip to Neuschwanstein Castle

Morning: Travel to Neuschwanstein Castle

On your fourth day, venture outside Munich for a day trip to Neuschwanstein Castle, one of the most famous castles in the world. Take a train or join a guided tour to reach the town of Füssen, where you can take a shuttle or hike up to the castle.

Afternoon: Explore Neuschwanstein and Hohenschwangau Castles

Tour the fairy-tale Neuschwanstein Castle, built by King Ludwig II, and learn about its fascinating history. If time permits, also visit the nearby Hohenschwangau Castle, Ludwig's childhood home. The surrounding area offers beautiful hiking trails and stunning views of the Bavarian Alps.

Evening: Return to Munich

Return to Munich in the evening and enjoy a relaxed dinner at a local restaurant, reflecting on the day's adventures.

Day 5: Munich's Hidden Gems and Relaxation

Morning: Deutsches Museum

Spend your final day in Munich exploring the Deutsches Museum, the largest science and technology museum in the world. With exhibits covering everything from aviation and space exploration to robotics and energy, the museum offers a fascinating look at human innovation. Don't miss the interactive exhibits and the planetarium.

Afternoon: Explore Munich's Hidden Gems

In the afternoon, take some time to explore some of Munich's lesser-known attractions. Visit the Asam Church, a stunning Baroque church tucked away in the city center, or the Lenbachhaus, an art museum dedicated to the Blue Rider movement. If you're a beer enthusiast, consider a visit to the Beer and Oktoberfest Museum for an insight into Munich's brewing traditions.

Evening: Farewell Dinner in the Glockenbachviertel

End your Munich adventure with a farewell dinner in the trendy Glockenbachviertel district. This area is known for its stylish bars, restaurants, and boutiques. Enjoy a final Bavarian meal or try one of the international cuisines that have made Munich's dining scene so diverse.

Tips for Your 5-Day Visit

- **Public Transportation:** Make use of Munich's efficient public transportation system to get around the city. Consider purchasing a 5-day Munich CityTourCard for unlimited travel and discounts on attractions.
- **Pace Yourself:** While there's plenty to see, don't forget to take breaks and enjoy the city's many parks, cafes, and beer gardens.
- **Weather Considerations:** Munich's weather can be variable, so pack accordingly and have a few indoor activities planned in case of rain.

C. 7-Day Munich and Surroundings Itinerary

Day 1: Introduction to Munich

Morning: Marienplatz and the Old Town

Start your week in Munich by immersing yourself in the heart of the city—Marienplatz. Watch the Glockenspiel in the New Town Hall as it brings Munich's history to life, then explore the surrounding Old Town. Visit the Frauenkirche, the iconic twin-towered cathedral, and St. Peter's Church, where you can climb the tower for a panoramic view of Munich.

Afternoon: Viktualienmarkt and Munich Residenz

After a leisurely lunch at Viktualienmarkt, Munich's famous food market, head to the Munich Residenz. Spend the afternoon touring the opulent state rooms, the Treasury, and the beautiful Hofgarten. This former royal palace offers a fascinating glimpse into Bavaria's regal past.

Evening: Traditional Bavarian Dinner

Conclude your first day with a traditional Bavarian dinner at a historic beer hall, such as the Hofbräuhaus or Augustiner Bräustuben. Enjoy hearty dishes like schnitzel or roast pork, accompanied by a refreshing stein of local beer.

Day 2: Art, Culture, and the English Garden

Morning: Museum Quarter (Kunstareal)

Dedicate your morning to exploring Munich's Museum Quarter, the Kunstareal. Choose from the

Alte Pinakothek, Neue Pinakothek, or the Pinakothek der Moderne, depending on your interests. These museums house some of Europe's finest collections of art, from Old Masters to modern masterpieces.

Afternoon: The English Garden

After a morning of art and culture, unwind in the English Garden, one of the largest urban parks in the world. Stroll through the park's picturesque landscapes, visit the Chinese Tower, and watch surfers ride the Eisbachwelle. Consider renting a paddleboat on the Kleinhesseloher See or relaxing in one of the park's beer gardens.

Evening: Schwabing District

In the evening, explore the lively Schwabing district, known for its artistic heritage and vibrant nightlife. Enjoy dinner at a local restaurant and perhaps catch some live music or simply soak in the atmosphere of this bohemian neighborhood.

Day 3: Nymphenburg Palace and Olympiapark

Morning: Nymphenburg Palace

Spend your morning exploring Nymphenburg Palace, the grand Baroque residence of the Bavarian royal family. Wander through the palace's opulent rooms, admire the expansive gardens, and visit the various pavilions, including the exquisite Amalienburg hunting lodge.

Afternoon: Olympiapark and BMW Museum

In the afternoon, visit Olympiapark, the site of the 1972 Summer Olympics. Explore the Olympic Stadium, take in the views from the Olympic Tower, and walk around the park's scenic grounds. Then, head to the nearby BMW Museum and BMW Welt to immerse yourself in the history and future of BMW, one of the world's most iconic automobile brands.

Evening: Dinner with a View

End your day with dinner at the revolving restaurant in the Olympic Tower, where you can enjoy gourmet cuisine while taking in panoramic views of Munich and beyond.

Day 4: Day Trip to Neuschwanstein Castle

Morning: Travel to Neuschwanstein Castle

On your fourth day, venture outside Munich for a day trip to Neuschwanstein Castle, the fairy-tale castle that inspired Disney's Sleeping Beauty Castle. Take a train or join a guided tour to reach the town of Füssen, where you can take a shuttle or hike up to the castle.

Afternoon: Explore Neuschwanstein and Hohenschwangau Castles

Tour the interior of Neuschwanstein Castle, marveling at its ornate rooms and breathtaking views of the surrounding mountains. If time permits, also visit the nearby Hohenschwangau Castle, King Ludwig II's childhood home. The area offers beautiful hiking trails and stunning vistas of the Bavarian Alps.

Evening: Return to Munich

Return to Munich in the evening and enjoy a relaxed dinner at a local restaurant, perhaps reflecting on the day's magical experiences.

Day 5: Day Trip to Salzburg or the Bavarian Alps

Option 1: Salzburg, Austria

Start your day with a scenic train ride to Salzburg, Austria, the birthplace of Mozart and the setting for "The Sound of Music." Explore the historic Old Town, visit Mozart's birthplace, and tour the stunning Hohensalzburg Fortress. Take a leisurely stroll through the Mirabell Gardens before returning to Munich in the evening.

Option 2: Bavarian Alps and Zugspitze

Alternatively, take a day trip to the Bavarian Alps. Travel to Garmisch-Partenkirchen and take the cable car up to the summit of Zugspitze, Germany's highest peak. Enjoy breathtaking views of the Alps and, if visiting in winter, consider some skiing or snowboarding. In the summer, the area offers excellent hiking opportunities. Return to Munich in the evening.

Day 6: Hidden Gems and Leisure

Morning: Deutsches Museum

Spend your morning exploring the Deutsches Museum, the largest science and technology museum in the world. With exhibits covering everything from aviation and space exploration to robotics and energy, the museum offers a fascinating look at human innovation. Interactive exhibits and the planetarium are highlights.

Afternoon: Explore Munich's Hidden Gems

In the afternoon, take time to discover some of Munich's lesser-known attractions. Visit the Asam Church, a stunning Baroque church tucked away in the city center, or explore the Lenbachhaus, an art museum dedicated to the Blue Rider movement. If you're interested in Munich's beer culture, visit the Beer and Oktoberfest Museum for an insightful and fun experience.

Evening: Glockenbachviertel District

Conclude your day with dinner in the trendy Glockenbachviertel district, known for its stylish bars, restaurants, and boutiques. This vibrant area is perfect for a relaxed evening out, whether you're in the mood for Bavarian cuisine or something more international.

Day 7: Munich's Surroundings or Leisure Day

Option 1: Day Trip to Dachau Concentration Camp Memorial Site

On your final day, take a sobering but important trip to the Dachau Concentration Camp Memorial Site. Located just outside Munich, Dachau was the first Nazi concentration camp and now serves as a memorial and museum. The site offers guided tours and exhibits that provide a deep understanding of this dark chapter in history. It's a profound experience that many visitors find essential during their time in Munich.

Option 2: Leisure Day in Munich

Alternatively, if you prefer a more relaxed final day, spend it exploring more of Munich at your own pace. Revisit your favorite spots, do some shopping in the city center, or simply enjoy the atmosphere of one of Munich's beautiful parks. Consider taking a leisurely boat ride on the Isar River or relaxing in one of the city's historic cafes.

Evening: Farewell Dinner in Munich

End your 7-day journey with a farewell dinner at one of Munich's finer restaurants. Treat yourself to a memorable dining experience at Tantris, a Michelin-starred restaurant known for its innovative cuisine, or enjoy a final Bavarian feast at Schwarzreiter Tagesbar & Restaurant. Reflect on the week's adventures and the many memories you've made.

Tips for Your 7-Day Visit

- **Public Transportation:** Munich's efficient public transportation system makes it easy to get around. Consider purchasing a Munich CityTourCard or Bayern-Ticket for unlimited travel within the city and day trips around Bavaria.
- **Flexible Scheduling:** With a full week, you have the flexibility to adjust your itinerary based on your interests and the weather. Don't hesitate to take a slower pace or spend more time in places that captivate you.
- **Seasonal Considerations:** Depending on the time of year, some activities (like hiking or skiing in the Alps) may be more suitable. Plan accordingly to make the most of Munich's seasonal offerings.

D. Tips for Customizing Your Own Itinerary

1. Prioritize Your Interests

Start by considering what excites you the most about Munich. Are you fascinated by history and architecture? Then you might want to focus on exploring the city's many historical sites, such as the Munich Residenz, Nymphenburg Palace, and the various churches and museums. If art and culture are your passions, dedicating time to the city's renowned museums like the Alte Pinakothek, Lenbachhaus, and the Deutsches Museum would be ideal.

For those who love the outdoors, Munich's parks, such as the English Garden and Olympiapark, offer beautiful green spaces to explore. And if food is a big part of your travel experience, be sure to include visits to traditional beer halls, markets like Viktualienmarkt, and perhaps even a Bavarian cooking class.

2. Consider Your Pace

Think about how you like to travel. Do you enjoy packing your days with activities, or do you prefer a more leisurely pace with time to relax and soak in the atmosphere? If you prefer a busy itinerary, you might pack multiple attractions into each day, ensuring you see as much as possible. On the other hand, if you like to take things slow, consider focusing on one or two major sites per day, with plenty of time for wandering, enjoying long meals, and spontaneous discoveries.

3. Balance Must-See Attractions with Hidden Gems

While it's important to visit Munich's top attractions like Marienplatz, the BMW Museum, and Neuschwanstein Castle, don't forget to leave room in your itinerary for exploring the city's lesser-known treasures. Munich is full of hidden gems, from small art galleries and unique boutiques to charming cafes and peaceful parks. Balancing well-known sites with off-the-beaten-path experiences will give you a richer and more personal perspective on the city.

4. Plan for Flexibility

Even the best-laid plans can change, so it's a good idea to build some flexibility into your itinerary. Weather, mood, or unexpected discoveries might lead you to adjust your plans. For example, if it starts raining, you might shift from outdoor activities to museum visits. Or, if you find a neighborhood you particularly love, give yourself the freedom to spend extra time there. Having a flexible itinerary allows you to adapt and make the most of your trip.

5. Make Time for Day Trips

Munich is ideally located for day trips to some of Bavaria's most beautiful and historic sites. Consider adding a day trip to Neuschwanstein Castle,

Salzburg, the Bavarian Alps, or even the picturesque towns along the Romantic Road. These excursions offer a chance to see more of the region and experience the stunning landscapes and cultural richness of Bavaria.

6. Utilize Public Transportation

Munich's public transportation system is efficient and easy to use, making it simple to get around the city and beyond. Plan your itinerary with the U-Bahn, S-Bahn, trams, and buses in mind. Purchasing a multi-day travel pass, such as the Munich CityTourCard or the Bayern-Ticket, can save you money and provide unlimited travel on public transport, as well as discounts on some attractions.

7. Embrace Seasonal Experiences

Depending on when you visit Munich, there may be seasonal events and activities that you won't want to miss. If you're visiting in late September or early October, for example, attending Oktoberfest should be high on your list. In winter, the Christmas markets (Christkindlmarkts) are a magical experience, with festive decorations, mulled wine, and handcrafted gifts. Summer visits are perfect for enjoying outdoor beer gardens, parks, and festivals. Tailor your itinerary to make the most of what Munich has to offer during your visit.

8. Book Key Attractions in Advance

To avoid disappointment, it's a good idea to book tickets for popular attractions and tours in advance, especially during peak tourist seasons. This is particularly important for sites like Neuschwanstein Castle, the BMW Museum, and guided tours of the Munich Residenz. Booking ahead not only guarantees your spot but can also save you time by allowing you to skip the lines.

9. Allow Time for Rest and Relaxation

While it's tempting to fill every moment with activities, remember to include time for rest and relaxation in your itinerary. Munich has plenty of places where you can unwind, from tranquil gardens like the Hofgarten and the English Garden to cozy cafes where you can enjoy a coffee and a slice of cake. Giving yourself time to relax will ensure you stay refreshed and enjoy your trip to the fullest.

10. Personalize Your Culinary Experiences

Food is a big part of Munich's culture, so be sure to plan some memorable dining experiences. Whether you want to sample traditional Bavarian dishes in a historic beer hall, enjoy fine dining at a Michelin-starred restaurant, or explore the city's burgeoning street food scene, tailor your meals to suit your tastes. Don't forget to try local specialties like Weisswurst, pretzels, and of course, Bavarian beer.

Chapter 6: Exploring Munich's Culture and History

A. Munich's Beer Culture

A Brief History of Munich's Beer Culture

Beer brewing in Munich dates back to the Middle Ages, with the city's first documented brewery, Weihenstephan Abbey, founded in 1040. Munich quickly became known for its high-quality beer, thanks in part to the Reinheitsgebot, or Bavarian Beer Purity Law, enacted in 1516. This law, which allowed only water, barley, and hops in the brewing process, ensured that Munich's beer maintained a standard of purity and excellence that is still celebrated today.

Munich is also the birthplace of some of the world's most famous beer styles, including the Märzen, a medium-bodied lager traditionally brewed in March, and the Weissbier, a refreshing wheat beer. These styles are still enjoyed in Munich's many beer halls and breweries, where tradition meets the vibrant social life of the city.

Must-Visit Breweries and Beer Halls

- **Hofbräuhaus München:** Perhaps the most famous beer hall in the world, Hofbräuhaus München has been serving beer since 1589. Originally founded by the Bavarian royal family, it's a lively place where visitors and locals gather to enjoy traditional Bavarian music, hearty food, and of course, liters of beer served in massive steins. The atmosphere is always festive, making it a must-visit for anyone wanting to experience Munich's beer culture.

- **Augustiner Bräustuben:** As Munich's oldest privately-owned brewery, Augustiner is a beloved institution. The beer hall at Landsberger Straße is a favorite among locals, known for its warm, unpretentious atmosphere. The Augustiner beer, brewed according to traditional methods, is often regarded as one of the best in the city. Pair it with a pretzel or roast pork for the full Bavarian experience.

- **Paulaner Bräuhaus:** Another historic brewery, Paulaner, offers a more modern take on the traditional beer hall experience. Located in the heart of the city, Paulaner Bräuhaus is known for its seasonal beers and welcoming ambiance. The beer is brewed on-site, ensuring that every glass is as fresh as it gets.

- **Hacker-Pschorr Bräuhaus:** Hacker-Pschorr combines history with innovation. The brewery, which dates back to 1417, offers a variety of classic and craft beers in a contemporary setting. The beer hall, located near the Theresienwiese, the site of Oktoberfest, is a great place to enjoy a meal and sample some of Munich's finest brews.

Bavarian Traditions and Festivals

Bavaria is a region steeped in rich traditions, and nowhere are these more vibrantly displayed than in Munich, its capital. From the lively festivals that draw millions of visitors to the time-honored customs passed down through generations, Bavarian traditions are an integral part of life in Munich. Whether you're visiting during the height of a festival or simply want to experience the everyday culture, immersing yourself in these traditions offers a deeper understanding of what makes Munich so special.

Oktoberfest: The Crown Jewel of Bavarian Festivals

When most people think of Bavarian traditions, Oktoberfest immediately comes to mind. Held annually in Munich from late September to the first weekend in October, Oktoberfest is the largest beer festival in the world, attracting over six million visitors each year. But Oktoberfest is more than just a beer-drinking event; it's a celebration of Bavarian culture, complete with traditional music, folk dances, and parades.

The festival began in 1810 to celebrate the marriage of Crown Prince Ludwig and Princess Therese of Saxe-Hildburghausen. It was such a success that it became an annual event, growing in size and scope over the centuries. Today, Oktoberfest features massive beer tents run by Munich's major breweries, each offering their own special brews for the occasion. Visitors don traditional Bavarian attire—lederhosen for men and dirndls for women—as they enjoy hearty Bavarian dishes like roast chicken, pretzels, and sausages.

Beyond the beer tents, Oktoberfest includes a funfair with rides, games, and attractions for all ages. The atmosphere is electric, filled with the sounds of brass bands, the clinking of steins, and the laughter of people from around the world coming together to celebrate.

Other Notable Bavarian Festivals

- **Starkbierzeit (Strong Beer Festival):** While Oktoberfest is the most famous, Munich's Starkbierzeit is a beloved local tradition that takes place during Lent.

Originating with the monks of the Paulaner monastery, who brewed strong beer to sustain themselves during fasting, Starkbierzeit is now celebrated with rich, malty brews that pack a punch—often with an alcohol content of 7% or more. Held in March, this festival is less crowded than Oktoberfest, offering a more intimate and authentic experience.

- **Kocherlball:** This early morning folk dance festival takes place in the English Garden every July. Dating back to the 19th century, when Munich's cooks, maids, and servants would gather before work to dance and socialize, the Kocherlball has been revived in modern times as a charming nod to the past. Participants don traditional attire and dance to live folk music as the sun rises—a magical experience that feels like stepping back in time.

- **Auer Dult:** Held three times a year at Mariahilfplatz, Auer Dult is a traditional Bavarian market fair that dates back over 700 years. Each Dult (May, July, and October) features stalls selling everything from pottery and antiques to sweets and snacks, along with amusement rides and games. It's a great place to experience local culture, sample traditional foods, and pick up unique souvenirs.

Bavarian Customs and Everyday Traditions

Beyond the festivals, everyday Bavarian traditions are deeply rooted in Munich's culture. You'll notice the importance of food and drink in social gatherings, whether at a beer hall, a local café, or a family dinner. Bavarians take pride in their regional cuisine, which includes staples like Weisswurst (white sausage), Brezen (pretzels), and Obatzda (a cheese spread made with Camembert and butter).

Another cherished tradition is the wearing of traditional clothing, or Tracht, especially during festivals and special occasions. Lederhosen and dirndls are not just costumes; they're a symbol of Bavarian identity and pride.

B. Art and Museums

The Kunstareal: Munich's Museum Quarter

The Kunstareal, Munich's Museum Quarter, is the city's cultural heart, home to some of the most significant art collections in Europe. Located in the Maxvorstadt district, this area is a must-visit for anyone interested in art and culture.

- **Alte Pinakothek:** One of the oldest galleries in the world, the Alte Pinakothek houses an extraordinary collection of European paintings from the 14th to the 18th centuries. Here, you can admire works by Old Masters such as Albrecht Dürer, Peter Paul Rubens, and Rembrandt. The gallery's grand halls and natural light create a serene environment for contemplating these timeless masterpieces.

- **Neue Pinakothek:** Just across the street, the Neue Pinakothek offers a contrast to its older counterpart, focusing on 19th-century art. The collection includes works by Romantic and Impressionist painters, including Caspar David Friedrich, Vincent van Gogh, and Claude Monet. This museum provides a fascinating journey through the artistic movements that shaped modern art.

- **Pinakothek der Moderne:** For those interested in contemporary art, design, and architecture, the Pinakothek der Moderne is a must-see. This vast museum brings together four major disciplines under one roof: modern art, graphic art, architecture, and design. From Picasso to Warhol, the museum's collection spans the 20th and 21st centuries, offering a comprehensive look at the evolution of modern creativity.

- **Museum Brandhorst:** Nearby, the Museum Brandhorst is dedicated to contemporary art, featuring works by artists like Cy Twombly, Andy Warhol, and Damien Hirst. The museum's striking modern architecture and vibrant collections make it a highlight of Munich's cultural landscape.

Lenbachhaus: The Blue Rider and Beyond

The Lenbachhaus, located in a historic villa, is another gem in Munich's art scene. This museum is renowned for its collection of works by the Blue Rider (Der Blaue Reiter) group, an early 20th-century expressionist movement founded by artists such as Wassily Kandinsky, Franz Marc, and Gabriele Münter. The museum's vibrant collection captures the spirit of innovation and experimentation that defined this influential group.

In addition to the Blue Rider works, the Lenbachhaus also features contemporary art and temporary exhibitions, making it a dynamic and engaging place to visit.

The Glyptothek and the State Antiquities Collection

For those with an interest in classical art and archaeology, the Glyptothek and the State Antiquities Collection offer a fascinating journey into the ancient world. The Glyptothek, located on Königsplatz, houses a remarkable collection of

Greek and Roman sculptures, including the famous Barberini Faun and the Medusa Rondanini. The museum's neoclassical architecture and peaceful courtyards provide a fitting backdrop for these ancient masterpieces.

Next door, the State Antiquities Collection (Antikensammlung) complements the Glyptothek with its collection of ancient pottery, jewelry, and small sculptures. Together, these museums offer a deep dive into the art and culture of antiquity.

Bavarian National Museum

To round out your cultural tour, visit the Bavarian National Museum, which showcases the rich artistic and cultural heritage of Bavaria. The museum's extensive collection includes everything from medieval armor and religious art to folk costumes and decorative arts. It's a comprehensive exploration of Bavarian history and craftsmanship, offering a deeper understanding of the region's cultural identity.

C. Historic Churches and Architecture

Frauenkirche (Cathedral of Our Dear Lady)

No exploration of Munich's historic churches is complete without a visit to the Frauenkirche, the city's iconic cathedral. Known for its twin onion-domed towers, which dominate Munich's skyline, the Frauenkirche is a symbol of the city and a masterpiece of Gothic architecture.

Built between 1468 and 1488, the Frauenkirche was designed to be a grand statement of faith and power, capable of holding 20,000 worshippers. Despite its imposing size, the interior is surprisingly simple and austere, reflecting the Gothic emphasis on height and light. The cathedral's most famous feature is the Devil's Footstep, a mysterious footprint near the entrance that, according to legend, was left by the devil himself.

The Frauenkirche also offers one of the best views in Munich. Visitors can climb one of the towers for a panoramic vista of the city, with the Alps visible on clear days. The cathedral's location in the heart of the city makes it an ideal starting point for exploring Munich's historic center.

St. Peter's Church (Peterskirche)

St. Peter's Church, affectionately known as "Old Peter," is the oldest church in Munich, dating back to the 12th century. Situated just a stone's throw from Marienplatz, St. Peter's has been a focal point of Munich's religious life for centuries.

The church's architecture is a blend of Gothic, Renaissance, and Baroque styles, the result of numerous renovations and reconstructions over the centuries. Inside, you'll find a stunning Baroque altar, intricate frescoes, and a collection of religious art. One of the most striking features is the gilded statue of St. Peter, holding the keys to heaven, which stands above the high altar.

For those up for a challenge, climbing the 299 steps to the top of St. Peter's tower is well worth the effort. The tower offers spectacular views over Marienplatz and the rest of the city, making it a popular spot for photographers and sightseers alike.

Asam Church (Asamkirche)

Tucked away on Sendlinger Straße, the Asam Church is one of Munich's most beautiful and ornate Baroque churches. Built in the 18th century by the Asam brothers, who were both artists, the church was originally intended as a private chapel. However, it was later opened to the public, and today it stands as a testament to the brothers' artistic genius.

The Asam Church is relatively small, but it is richly decorated with elaborate stucco work, frescoes, and gilded details that create a sense of opulence and grandeur. The ceiling fresco, which depicts the life of St. John of Nepomuk, is particularly impressive, showcasing the Baroque love of drama and movement. Despite its small size, the church's interior feels expansive and awe-inspiring, drawing visitors into its intricate details and spiritual ambiance.

Theatiner Church (Theatinerkirche St. Kajetan)

Located on Odeonsplatz, the Theatiner Church is a striking example of Italian Baroque architecture in Munich. Built in the 17th century by Elector Ferdinand Maria and his wife, Henriette Adelaide, in gratitude for the birth of their son, the church was designed by Italian architects who brought a piece of Rome to Bavaria.

The Theatiner Church is instantly recognizable by its bright yellow façade and its impressive dome, which towers above the surrounding buildings. Inside, the church is filled with light, thanks to its white stucco walls and high ceilings. The ornate altars, sculptures, and tombs reflect the Baroque emphasis on grandeur and divine light, making it a beautiful and peaceful place to visit.

The church also has a significant historical connection, as it houses the tombs of several members of the Wittelsbach family, including King Maximilian II of Bavaria. Its location on Odeonsplatz makes it easily accessible, and it's often included in walking tours of Munich's historic center.

Michaelskirche (St. Michael's Church)

St. Michael's Church, located on Neuhauser Straße, is the largest Renaissance church north of the Alps and one of the most important examples of Renaissance architecture in Bavaria. Built between 1583 and 1597 by Duke Wilhelm V, the church was intended to serve as a symbol of the Counter-Reformation and the power of the Catholic Church.

The church's façade, with its statues of archangels and saints, is imposing and grand, while the interior is equally impressive, featuring a high vaulted ceiling, a grand altar, and a beautiful choir. The crypt of St. Michael's is the final resting place of several members of the Wittelsbach dynasty, including King Ludwig II, known for his fairy-tale castles.

St. Michael's Church is not only a place of worship but also a symbol of Munich's resilience and faith. It was heavily damaged during World War II but was meticulously restored to its former glory, making it a powerful testament to the city's history and spirit.

D. World War II and Munich's Dark Past

The Birthplace of the Nazi Movement

Munich is often referred to as the "Capital of the Movement" because it was here that Adolf Hitler and the Nazi Party first rose to power. The city was the site of many key events in the early years of the Nazi movement, including the Beer Hall Putsch in 1923, where Hitler attempted to overthrow the Weimar Republic government. Although the coup failed, it set the stage for Hitler's eventual rise to power.

One of the most significant locations from this period is the Hofbräuhaus, where the Nazi Party held its first mass meeting in 1920. Today, the Hofbräuhaus is a popular beer hall, but it also serves as a reminder of its complex history. Nearby, the Feldherrnhalle on Odeonsplatz, where the coup ended in a deadly confrontation with the police, stands as another historic site tied to the Nazi movement.

Dachau Concentration Camp Memorial Site

A visit to the Dachau Concentration Camp Memorial Site, located just outside Munich, is a deeply moving experience that highlights the atrocities committed during the Holocaust. Opened in 1933, Dachau was the first concentration camp established by the Nazi regime and served as a model for all subsequent camps. Over 200,000 prisoners were held here during its operation, and tens of thousands died due to the inhumane conditions.

Today, the site serves as a memorial and a place of education. Visitors can explore the preserved barracks, the crematorium, and the museum, which provides detailed accounts of life in the camp, the stories of the victims, and the horrors of the Holocaust. The memorial site also includes the International Monument, dedicated to the memory of those who suffered and died at Dachau.

The Documentation Center for the History of National Socialism

Located on the site of the former headquarters of the Nazi Party, the Documentation Center for the History of National Socialism is one of Munich's most important educational institutions dedicated to this dark period. The center provides a comprehensive overview of the rise of the Nazi Party, the impact of the regime on Munich and its citizens, and the atrocities committed during World War II.

The exhibitions include photographs, documents, and multimedia presentations that trace the history of National Socialism from its origins to its downfall. The center also addresses the post-war period and how Munich has dealt with its Nazi past. Visiting the Documentation Center is essential for those who wish to understand the full impact of the Nazi regime on Munich and Germany as a whole.

White Rose Memorial and the University of Munich

The White Rose was a resistance group composed mainly of students from the University of Munich who opposed the Nazi regime. Led by siblings Hans and Sophie Scholl, the group distributed leaflets that called for active opposition to Hitler and the Nazis. In 1943, Hans and Sophie Scholl, along with other members of the group, were arrested and executed for their resistance activities.

Today, the **University of Munich** honors the memory of the White Rose with a memorial in the atrium where the Scholls distributed their final leaflets. The pavement outside the university's main building is embedded with leaflets as a tribute to the bravery and sacrifice of these young resistors. The White Rose Memorial is a poignant reminder of the courage of those who stood against tyranny, even in the face of overwhelming danger.

Munich's Post-War Reconstruction and Remembrance

After the war, Munich faced the daunting task of rebuilding and coming to terms with its role in the events that led to the devastation of Germany and Europe. The city was heavily bombed during the war, and much of its historic architecture was destroyed. However, in the post-war period, Munich was meticulously reconstructed, with efforts to restore many of its historic buildings to their former glory.

The city has also made significant efforts to acknowledge and educate future generations about its Nazi past. Plaques, memorials, and educational programs throughout Munich serve as reminders of the city's history and the importance of remembering the victims of the Nazi regime.

Reflecting on Munich's Dark Past

While exploring Munich's darker history can be challenging, it is an essential part of understanding the city's identity and the broader historical context of World War II. Visiting these sites allows us to reflect on the consequences of hatred, intolerance, and authoritarianism, and underscores the importance of vigilance in defending democratic values and human rights.

Chapter 7: Food and Drink in Munich

A. Traditional Bavarian Cuisine

The Foundations of Bavarian Cuisine

Bavarian cuisine is deeply influenced by the agricultural heritage of the region. Historically, the people of Bavaria relied on ingredients that were readily available from local farms, forests, and rivers. This connection to the land is evident in the dishes that define Bavarian cooking—meats, root vegetables, dairy products, and hearty grains all play a central role.

One of the hallmarks of Bavarian cuisine is its emphasis on simplicity and comfort. The dishes are designed to be filling and nourishing, perfect for fueling a day of work or enjoying with friends and family. At the same time, Bavarian food is often accompanied by a sense of occasion, particularly when paired with the region's famous beers.

Key Ingredients in Bavarian Cooking

- **Meat:** Pork is the most common meat in Bavarian cuisine, featured in many iconic dishes. Sausages, roasts, and schnitzels are popular, and pork knuckle (Schweinshaxe) is a beloved specialty. Beef and veal are also commonly used, particularly in dishes like Sauerbraten (marinated pot roast) and Wiener Schnitzel.

- **Bread and Pretzels:** Bread is a staple in Bavarian meals, and you'll find a wide variety of breads and rolls served with most dishes. The iconic Brezen (pretzel) is a must-try, often enjoyed with mustard and Weisswurst (white sausage) or simply on its own as a snack.

- **Dairy:** Bavaria is known for its dairy products, particularly cheese and butter. Obatzda, a creamy cheese spread made with Camembert, butter, and paprika, is a popular dish served with bread or pretzels. Bavarians also love their desserts, many of which feature rich cream and custard.

- **Potatoes and Dumplings:** Potatoes are a key ingredient in Bavarian cuisine, prepared in various forms such as potato salad (Kartoffelsalat), mashed potatoes, and roasted potatoes. Dumplings (Knödel) made from bread or potatoes are also a classic side dish, often served with meats and gravies.

- **Cabbage and Sauerkraut:** Cabbage is another staple, whether it's served as Sauerkraut (fermented cabbage) alongside sausages or as Blaukraut (red cabbage) with roast pork. These dishes add a tangy and refreshing contrast to the richness of the meats.

Signature Bavarian Dishes

- **Weisswurst:** This traditional white sausage is made from veal and pork, flavored with parsley, lemon, and cardamom. It's typically served in the morning, often with sweet mustard and a pretzel. Weisswurst is a breakfast staple in Munich, and it's traditionally eaten before noon.

- **Schweinshaxe:** A hearty and flavorful dish, Schweinshaxe is a roasted pork knuckle with crispy skin and tender, juicy meat. It's often served with potato dumplings and gravy, making it a favorite at beer halls and traditional restaurants.

- **Wiener Schnitzel:** While originally from Austria, Wiener Schnitzel is a beloved dish in Bavaria as well. This breaded and fried veal cutlet is served with lemon wedges and is often accompanied by potato salad or lingonberry sauce.

- **Brezn and Obatzda:** This classic Bavarian snack combines a freshly baked pretzel with Obatzda, a savory cheese spread made with Camembert, butter, and spices. It's a popular choice in beer gardens and perfect for sharing with friends over a stein of beer.

- **Leberkäse:** Often described as a type of meatloaf, Leberkäse is made from finely ground pork and beef, baked until it forms a crispy crust. It's typically served in thick slices, either on its own or in a sandwich with mustard.

Where to Experience Traditional Bavarian Cuisine

- **Hofbräuhaus:** No visit to Munich is complete without a meal at Hofbräuhaus, the city's most famous beer hall. Here, you can enjoy classic Bavarian dishes like Schweinshaxe and Weisswurst in a lively and historic setting.

- **Augustiner Bräustuben:** This traditional beer hall is a local favorite, known for its authentic Bavarian cuisine and welcoming atmosphere. The Augustiner beer, served here fresh from the brewery, pairs perfectly with dishes like pork roast and dumplings.

- **Andechser am Dom:** Located near the Frauenkirche, Andechser am Dom offers a more intimate setting for enjoying Bavarian cuisine. The menu features a range of traditional dishes, including Schnitzel and Leberkäse, with an emphasis on high-quality ingredients.

- **Viktualienmarkt:** For a more casual experience, head to Viktualienmarkt, Munich's famous food market. Here, you can sample a variety of Bavarian specialties, from pretzels and sausages to cheese and pastries, while enjoying the lively market atmosphere.

B. Top Restaurants in Munich

1. Tantris

- **Location:** Johann-Fichte-Straße 7, 80805 Munich
- **History:** Opened in 1971, Tantris is a culinary institution in Munich, known for being a pioneer of fine dining in Germany.

The restaurant's name, inspired by Indian mythology, reflects its unique and spiritual approach to gastronomy. Tantris was one of the first restaurants in Germany to receive two Michelin stars, and it remains a beacon of haute cuisine.

- **How to Reach:** Easily accessible by U-Bahn, take the U6 to Dietlindenstraße, and it's a short walk from there.
- **What to Expect:** Expect a luxurious dining experience, with dishes that are as much about art as they are about taste. The seasonal menus are meticulously crafted, blending classic French techniques with innovative twists.
- **Cost:** A meal here is an investment in culinary excellence, with prices averaging around €200 per person for a tasting menu.
- **Booking:** Reservations are essential and can be made through their website at [tantris.de](https://www.tantris.de).
- **Opening Hours:** Tuesday to Saturday, 12:00 PM - 2:00 PM, 7:00 PM - 10:00 PM.

2. Dallmayr

- **Location:** Dienerstraße 14-15, 80331 Munich

- **History:** Dallmayr has been synonymous with luxury since the 1700s, originally known as a gourmet delicatessen. The restaurant, located above the famous food hall, offers an elegant setting with a menu that celebrates the finest ingredients.
- **How to Reach:** Situated in the heart of Munich, it's a short walk from Marienplatz, the city's central square.
- **What to Expect:** Dallmayr is a celebration of seasonal and regional products. The menu changes regularly, but always reflects a deep respect for Bavarian culinary traditions.
- **Cost:** Dining here is an indulgent experience, with a multi-course meal costing around €150 per person.
- **Booking:** Reservations are highly recommended and can be made through their website at [dallmayr.com](https://www.dallmayr.com).
- **Opening Hours:** Monday to Saturday, 11:30 AM - 2:30 PM, 6:00 PM - 10:00 PM.

3. Broeding

- **Location:** Schulstraße 9, 80634 Munich
- **History:** Broeding has built a reputation as one of Munich's most innovative restaurants since it opened in 1990. What sets Broeding apart is its commitment to a single

six-course menu each night, focusing on the freshest local ingredients.

- **How to Reach:** Located in the Neuhausen district, it's a quick tram ride on Line 12 to Albrechtstraße, followed by a short walk.
- **What to Expect:** This intimate dining spot offers a warm, welcoming atmosphere where the food is the star. The menu is a surprise each night, carefully crafted and paired with excellent Austrian wines.
- **Cost:** The six-course menu is reasonably priced at around €85 per person.
- **Booking:** Given its popularity and limited seating, reservations are essential. Book through their website at [broeding.de](https://www.broeding.de).
- **Opening Hours:** Monday to Saturday, 6:30 PM - 11:00 PM.

4. Hofbräuhaus

- **Location:** Platzl 9, 80331 Munich
- **History:** No visit to Munich is complete without a meal at the historic Hofbräuhaus. Founded in 1589, it's one of the world's

most famous beer halls and a symbol of Bavarian hospitality.

- **How to Reach:** Centrally located near Marienplatz, it's easily accessible by foot or public transport.
- **What to Expect:** Hofbräuhaus is about more than just food; it's an experience. Enjoy hearty Bavarian dishes like Schweinshaxe (pork knuckle) or Weisswurst (white sausage) in a lively atmosphere with traditional music.
- **Cost:** Surprisingly affordable, with main dishes ranging from €15 to €25.
- **Booking:** While you can just walk in, it's wise to reserve a table, especially during peak tourist seasons. Visit [hofbraeuhaus.de](https://www.hofbraeuhaus.de) for reservations.
- **Opening Hours:** Daily, 9:00 AM - 12:00 AM.

5. Atelier

SCAN THE QR CODE

1. Open your device camera app.
2. Position the QR code in the camera frame.
3. Hold your phone steady.
4. Wait for the code to be recognized.
5. Once recognized, tap on the notification or follow the prompt to access the content or action associated with the Qr code

- **Location:** Promenadeplatz 2-6, 80333 Munich (inside the Bayerischer Hof hotel)
- **History:** Atelier is a Michelin-starred restaurant that has earned international

acclaim for its creative approach to fine dining. Located in the prestigious Bayerischer Hof hotel, it offers a refined and intimate dining experience.

- **How to Reach:** Situated near Odeonsplatz, it's a short walk or U-Bahn ride from most central locations.
- **What to Expect:** Atelier is known for its modern European cuisine, with an emphasis on creativity and artistic presentation. The dishes here are as visually stunning as they are delicious.
- **Cost:** A meal at Atelier is a splurge, with tasting menus starting at €195 per person.
- **Booking:** Reservations are essential and can be made through their website at [bayerischerhof.de](https://www.bayerischerhof.de).
- **Opening Hours:** Tuesday to Saturday, 6:30 PM - 9:00 PM.

C. Must-Try Dishes and Where to Find Them

1. Weisswurst (White Sausage)

What It Is: Weisswurst is a traditional Bavarian sausage made from finely minced veal and pork, flavored with parsley, lemon, and cardamom. It's distinctively pale in color and is traditionally served in a bowl of hot water to keep it warm. Weisswurst is typically eaten in the morning and is accompanied by sweet mustard (Weißwurstsenf) and freshly baked pretzels.

Where to Try It:
- **Weisses Bräuhaus:** Located in the heart of Munich, Weisses Bräuhaus is renowned for its Weisswurst. This historic beer hall has been serving up Bavarian specialties since 1540, making it the perfect place to try this classic dish.
- **Hofbräuhaus:** Another iconic location, Hofbräuhaus serves Weisswurst daily, offering an authentic experience in a lively atmosphere. Enjoy your sausage with a stein of Hofbräu beer.

2. Schweinshaxe (Pork Knuckle)

What It Is: Schweinshaxe is a roasted pork knuckle, known for its crispy skin and tender, flavorful meat. The dish is typically slow-cooked to achieve the perfect balance of textures. It's often served with potato dumplings (Knödel) and Sauerkraut or red cabbage (Blaukraut).

Where to Try It:
- **Augustiner Bräustuben:** This traditional beer hall is famous for its Schweinshaxe. The portions are generous, and the dish is paired perfectly with Augustiner beer, one of Munich's oldest and most beloved brews.
- **Haxnbauer:** As the name suggests, Haxnbauer specializes in roasted pork

knuckle. Located near Marienplatz, this restaurant offers a cozy, rustic setting where you can enjoy one of the best Schweinshaxe in Munich.

3. Wiener Schnitzel

What It Is: While originally an Austrian dish, Wiener Schnitzel is a staple in Bavarian cuisine. It consists of a breaded and fried veal cutlet, traditionally served with a slice of lemon, potato salad, or lingonberry sauce.

Where to Try It:
- **Andechser am Dom:** This popular restaurant near the Frauenkirche serves a delicious Wiener Schnitzel in a warm and welcoming environment. Their version is crispy on the outside and tender on the inside, paired with classic Bavarian sides.
- **Zum Franziskaner:** A long-standing favorite among locals, Zum Franziskaner offers an excellent Wiener Schnitzel. The restaurant's traditional Bavarian decor adds to the overall dining experience.

4. Brezn and Obatzda

What It Is: Brezn (pretzels) are a quintessential part of Bavarian cuisine, often enjoyed with Obatzda, a savory cheese spread made from Camembert, butter, and spices. This combination is a popular snack in beer gardens and pairs perfectly with a cold beer.

Where to Try It:
- **Hirschgarten:** Known as one of the largest beer gardens in Europe, Hirschgarten is the perfect place to enjoy a pretzel with Obatzda. The relaxed outdoor setting and lively atmosphere make for an authentic Bavarian experience.
- **Viktualienmarkt:** At Munich's famous food market, you can find fresh pretzels and Obatzda at various stalls. Grab a seat at one of the communal tables and enjoy your snack while people-watching in this bustling market.

5. Leberkäse

What It Is: Leberkäse, often compared to meatloaf, is a finely ground mixture of pork and beef, baked until it forms a crispy crust. It's typically served in thick slices, either on its own, with mustard, or in a sandwich (Leberkässemmel).

Where to Try It:
- **Leberkäs Wimmer:** This popular chain specializes in Leberkäse, offering various flavors and styles. It's an ideal spot for a quick and tasty Leberkässemmel, perfect for a snack on the go.
- **Dallmayr:** Known for its high-quality delicatessen, Dallmayr offers a gourmet

version of Leberkäse. Located near
Marienplatz, it's a great place to try this
Bavarian specialty with a touch of elegance.

6. Kaiserschmarrn

What It Is: Kaiserschmarrn is a traditional
Bavarian dessert, a fluffy shredded pancake often
served with powdered sugar, raisins, and a side of
fruit compote, usually applesauce or plum sauce.
This dish is sweet, filling, and perfect for those with
a sweet tooth.

Where to Try It:
- **Café Frischhut:** Known as one of Munich's
  best spots for traditional pastries and
  desserts, Café Frischhut offers a delightful
  Kaiserschmarrn in a cozy and nostalgic
  setting.
- **Café Luitpold:** Located in the heart of
  Munich, Café Luitpold is an elegant café
  where you can enjoy a sophisticated version
  of Kaiserschmarrn, perfect for a
  mid-afternoon treat.

D. Beer Gardens and Beer Halls

The Tradition of Beer Gardens

Beer gardens (Biergärten) are an essential part of
Munich's cultural landscape, dating back to the
early 19th century. Originally, they were created by
breweries to store beer in cool cellars during the

summer months, with outdoor seating provided for customers to enjoy the beer on-site. Today, beer gardens are synonymous with relaxation and conviviality, offering a laid-back setting where you can enjoy a refreshing drink and hearty Bavarian food.

- **Hirschgarten:** Located in the district of Nymphenburg, Hirschgarten is the largest beer garden in Munich and possibly the largest in the world, with seating for over 8,000 guests. Set in a picturesque park with deer roaming nearby, Hirschgarten offers a quintessential beer garden experience. You can bring your own food or purchase traditional Bavarian fare from the vendors on-site. Pair your meal with a cold Maß (liter) of Augustiner beer, and you'll be living like a true Münchner.

- **Chinesischer Turm (Chinese Tower):** Situated in the heart of the English Garden, this iconic beer garden is one of the most popular in Munich. The Chinese Tower itself is a pagoda-style structure that adds a unique flair to the setting. With live brass band music and a lively atmosphere, it's a favorite spot for both locals and visitors. Traditional Bavarian dishes like Hendl (roast chicken) and Brezn (pretzels) are readily available, making it easy to enjoy a classic Bavarian meal with your beer.

The Historic Beer Halls of Munich

Beer halls (Bierhallen) offer a more traditional indoor setting, often housed in historic buildings with grand interiors that reflect the city's rich brewing history. These beer halls are the beating heart of Munich's social life, where people come together to celebrate, socialize, and, of course, drink beer.

- **Hofbräuhaus:** Perhaps the most famous beer hall in the world, Hofbräuhaus dates back to 1589 and was originally established as the royal brewery of the Kingdom of Bavaria. Today, it is a must-visit destination for anyone coming to Munich. The beer hall is massive, with a main hall that seats hundreds and a charming beer garden in the courtyard. Hofbräuhaus serves its signature Hofbräu beer, alongside classic Bavarian dishes like Schweinshaxe (pork knuckle) and Weisswurst (white sausage). The lively atmosphere, complete with traditional Bavarian music, makes every visit a celebration.

- **Augustiner Bräustuben:** Another historic beer hall, Augustiner Bräustuben is known for its authentic Bavarian ambiance and excellent beer, brewed by the Augustiner Brewery, Munich's oldest privately-owned brewery. The beer hall is less touristy than Hofbräuhaus, offering a more local experience. The beer is served from wooden barrels, and the menu features a variety of Bavarian specialties, including Obatzda (cheese spread) and Leberkäse (Bavarian meatloaf).

The Unique Atmosphere

What sets Munich's beer gardens and beer halls apart is the unique atmosphere of Gemütlichkeit—a German word that doesn't have a direct English translation but roughly means a sense of warmth, friendliness, and good cheer. In these spaces, the beer is important, but the company and the experience are what make the visit truly special. Whether you're sitting at a long wooden table in a beer hall or under the dappled shade of a beer garden, you'll find yourself surrounded by laughter, conversation, and the clinking of steins—a true taste of Bavarian life.

E. Fine Dining and International Cuisine

Tantris

History and Overview:
Tantris is one of Munich's most iconic Michelin-starred restaurants, renowned for its innovative approach to French cuisine. Established in 1971, Tantris has long been a cornerstone of Munich's fine dining scene, offering a unique combination of bold design and culinary excellence.

What to Do There:
Enjoy a multi-course tasting menu that showcases seasonal ingredients prepared with artistic flair. The menu changes regularly, but expect dishes like lobster with chanterelles or veal with truffle sauce, each paired with an exquisite selection of wines.

Where to Stay Nearby:
For a convenient stay, consider the Hotel Biederstein am Englischen Garten. This boutique hotel is a short drive from Tantris and offers comfortable rooms with a modern touch.

Contact and Booking Information:
- **Address:** Johann-Fichte-Straße 7, 80805 Munich
- **Phone:** +49 89 3619590
- **Website:** www.tantris.de
- **Cost:** Expect to pay around €180-€250 per person for the tasting menu.
- **Best Time to Visit:** Dinner service, especially on weekends. Reservations are essential.
- **How to Get There:** Tantris is located in the Schwabing district. It's accessible via the U-Bahn; the nearest station is **Alte Heide** on the U6 line.

Atelier

History and Overview:

Located in the luxurious Bayerischer Hof hotel, Atelier is a Michelin-starred restaurant that offers a sophisticated dining experience with a focus on contemporary European cuisine.

What to Do There:
Dine on artfully crafted dishes in an intimate setting. The seasonal tasting menu may include dishes like venison with beetroot and elderflower or turbot with caviar. The restaurant's elegant atmosphere makes it perfect for special occasions.

Where to Stay Nearby:
Staying at the **Bayerischer Hof** itself is an excellent option, offering luxurious accommodations and easy access to the city's attractions.

Contact and Booking Information:
- **Address:** Promenadepl. 2-6, 80333 Munich
- **Phone:** +49 89 2120995
- **Website:** www.bayerischerhof.de
- **Cost:** Approximately €200-€300 per person for the tasting menu.
- **Best Time to Visit:** Dinner service. Reservations are required well in advance.
- **How to Get There:** Atelier is located in central Munich, near Marienplatz. It's easily accessible by U-Bahn, with Marienplatz station nearby.

Matsuhisa Munich

History and Overview:
Matsuhisa Munich, located in the Mandarin Oriental hotel, is part of the global chain created by celebrity chef Nobu Matsuhisa. The restaurant specializes in Japanese-Peruvian fusion cuisine, offering a unique dining experience in the heart of Munich.

What to Do There:
Savor signature dishes such as black cod miso and yellowtail jalapeño, combining Japanese techniques with Peruvian flavors. The sleek, modern ambiance complements the innovative menu.

Where to Stay Nearby:
Stay at the Mandarin Oriental, Munich, where you can enjoy luxurious accommodations and world-class amenities.

Contact and Booking Information:
- **Address:** Neuturmstraße 1, 80331 Munich
- **Phone:** +49 89 290980
- **Website:** www.mandarinoriental.com
- **Cost:** Approximately €150-€250 per person.
- **Best Time to Visit:** Dinner service. Reservations are recommended.
- **How to Get There:** Located in the Altstadt-Lehel district, Matsuhisa is easily

accessible via the U-Bahn, with the Marienplatz station a short walk away.

Cocoon

History and Overview:
Cocoon is a trendy Italian restaurant located in the Glockenbachviertel district. Known for its modern take on Italian classics, Cocoon offers a stylish dining experience with a focus on fresh, high-quality ingredients.

What to Do There:
Enjoy a menu that features handmade pasta, seafood risotto, and other Italian delicacies. The restaurant's contemporary design and vibrant atmosphere make it a popular spot for both locals and visitors.

Where to Stay Nearby:
Consider staying at Hotel Deutsche Eiche, a boutique hotel in the Glockenbachviertel area, known for its friendly service and comfortable rooms.

Contact and Booking Information:
- **Address:** Thalkirchner Str. 2, 80337 Munich
- **Phone:** +49 89 51777122
- **Website:** www.cocoon-restaurant.de
- **Cost:** Approximately €40-€70 per person.

- **Best Time to Visit:** Dinner service. Reservations are recommended, especially on weekends.
- **How to Get There:** Located in the lively Glockenbachviertel, Cocoon is accessible via the U-Bahn, with the Sendlinger Tor station nearby.

Kismet

History and Overview:
Kismet is a chic Middle Eastern restaurant located in the Maxvorstadt district. The restaurant offers a vibrant menu inspired by the flavors of the Levant, with an emphasis on fresh ingredients and bold spices.

What to Do There:
Indulge in a variety of mezze plates, grilled meats, and vegetarian options. The lively atmosphere and stylish decor make Kismet a great spot for a relaxed yet sophisticated dining experience.

Where to Stay Nearby:
Hotel Europa offers comfortable accommodations within walking distance of Kismet, making it a convenient choice for travelers.

Contact and Booking Information:
- **Address:** Türkenstraße 84, 80799 Munich
- **Phone:** +49 89 28803630

- **Website:**
  [www.kismet-muenchen.de](https://www.kis met-muenchen.de)
- **Cost:** Approximately €30-€60 per person.
- **Best Time to Visit:** Dinner service. Reservations are advisable.
- **How to Get There:** Kismet is located in Maxvorstadt, easily reachable by public transport. The nearest U-Bahn station is Universität, on the U3/U6 lines.

F. Cafés and Bakeries

Café Frischhut (Schmalznudel)

History and Overview:
Café Frischhut, also known as Schmalznudel, is a beloved institution in Munich, famous for its traditional Bavarian pastries. Established in 1973, this café has become a go-to spot for locals and tourists alike who crave freshly fried doughnuts and other sweet treats.

What to Do There:
Don't miss the café's signature Schmalznudel, a type of deep-fried dough that's crispy on the outside and soft on the inside. Pair it with a strong coffee or hot chocolate for the perfect morning or afternoon snack.

Where to Stay Nearby:
Stay at Hotel Mercure München Altstadt, which is just a short walk from Café Frischhut. This hotel

offers modern amenities and a convenient location in the heart of the city.

Contact and Booking Information:
- **Address:** Prälat-Zistl-Straße 8, 80331 Munich
- **Phone:** +49 89 26023156
- **Website:** www.frischhut.de
- **Cost:** Pastries start at around €2, with coffee priced around €3.
- **Best Time to Visit:** Early morning or late afternoon when the pastries are freshly made.
- **How to Get There:** Café Frischhut is located near Viktualienmarkt and is easily accessible by U-Bahn; the nearest station is Marienplatz.

Café Luitpold

History and Overview:
Café Luitpold is one of Munich's grandest and most historic cafés, dating back to 1888. Known for its elegant atmosphere and exquisite pastries, Café Luitpold has been a gathering place for artists, intellectuals, and locals for over a century.

What to Do There:
Indulge in a slice of their famous Prinzregententorte, a classic Bavarian cake made with multiple layers of sponge cake and chocolate

buttercream. The café also offers a wide selection of other cakes, pastries, and chocolates, all made on-site.

Where to Stay Nearby:
Consider staying at Hotel Bayerischer Hof, one of Munich's most luxurious hotels, located just a short stroll from Café Luitpold.

Contact and Booking Information:
- **Address:** Brienner Str. 11, 80333 Munich
- **Phone:** +49 89 2428750
- **Website:** www.cafe-luitpold.de
- **Cost:** Cakes and pastries start at around €4, with coffee priced around €4-€5.
- **Best Time to Visit:** Mid-afternoon is perfect for enjoying a slice of cake with coffee in a relaxed atmosphere.
- **How to Get There:** Café Luitpold is centrally located in Munich, close to the Odeonsplatz U-Bahn station.

Rischart

History and Overview:
Rischart is a well-known bakery chain in Munich, with several locations throughout the city. Established in 1883, Rischart is celebrated for its high-quality baked goods, including breads, pastries, and cakes.

What to Do There:
Try their classic Bavarian pretzels or one of their many cakes, such as the Käsesahnetorte (cheesecake) or Apfelstrudel (apple strudel). Rischart is also a great spot for picking up fresh bread or a quick snack while exploring the city.

Where to Stay Nearby:
Stay at Hotel Deutsche Eiche, conveniently located near several Rischart locations, including the one at Viktualienmarkt.

Contact and Booking Information:
- **Address:** Multiple locations, including Viktualienmarkt 2, 80331 Munich
- **Phone:** +49 89 23778-0
- **Website:** www.rischart.de
- **Cost:** Pastries and snacks start at around €2, with coffee priced around €3.
- **Best Time to Visit:** Anytime during the day, particularly if you're looking for a quick bite while shopping or sightseeing.
- **How to Get There:** Rischart's main location at Viktualienmarkt is easily accessible by U-Bahn, with Marienplatz station nearby.

Café Glockenspiel

History and Overview:
Café Glockenspiel is a stylish café located on the fifth floor of a building overlooking Marienplatz. Known for its stunning views of the Glockenspiel

and the Frauenkirche, this café offers a delightful combination of ambiance, great coffee, and delicious cakes.

What to Do There:
Enjoy a leisurely breakfast or afternoon coffee while taking in the panoramic views of Munich's most famous square. Their cakes, particularly the apple cake and raspberry tart, are crowd favorites.

Where to Stay Nearby:
For a central location, stay at Hotel Schlicker, which is just a short walk from Café Glockenspiel and offers comfortable accommodations in the heart of Munich.

Contact and Booking Information:
- **Address:** Marienplatz 28, 80331 Munich
- **Phone:** +49 89 264256
- **Website:** www.cafe-glockenspiel.de
- **Cost:** Cakes and pastries start at around €4, with coffee priced around €4-€5.
- **Best Time to Visit:** Visit in the morning for breakfast or in the afternoon for coffee and cake with a view.
- **How to Get There:** Café Glockenspiel is located directly on Marienplatz, accessible via the Marienplatz U-Bahn station.

Café Frischhut

History and Overview:
Café Frischhut, also known as Schmalznudel, is a beloved institution in Munich, famous for its traditional Bavarian pastries. Established in 1973, this café has become a go-to spot for locals and tourists alike who crave freshly fried doughnuts and other sweet treats.

What to Do There:
Don't miss the café's signature Schmalznudel, a type of deep-fried dough that's crispy on the outside and soft on the inside. Pair it with a strong coffee or hot chocolate for the perfect morning or afternoon snack.

Where to Stay Nearby:
Stay at Hotel Mercure München Altstadt, which is just a short walk from Café Frischhut. This hotel offers modern amenities and a convenient location in the heart of the city.

Contact and Booking Information:
- **Address:** Prälat-Zistl-Straße 8, 80331 Munich
- **Phone:** +49 89 26023156
- **Website:** www.frischhut.de
- **Cost:** Pastries start at around €2, with coffee priced around €3.
- **Best Time to Visit:** Early morning or late afternoon when the pastries are freshly made.

- **How to Get There:** Café Frischhut is located near Viktualienmarkt and is easily accessible by U-Bahn; the nearest station is Marienplatz.

Chapter 8: Shopping in Munich

A. High-End Shopping

1. Maximilianstraße

Maximilianstraße is Munich's premier shopping street, often compared to Paris's Champs-Élysées or London's Bond Street. Located in the city center, this elegant boulevard is lined with a mix of historical buildings and modern architecture, creating a refined backdrop for some of the world's most prestigious brands.

What to Expect:
On Maximilianstraße, you'll find flagship stores from international luxury brands such as Louis Vuitton, Gucci, Prada, Chanel, and Dior. These boutiques offer the latest in high fashion, from ready-to-wear collections to exclusive accessories. Whether you're window shopping or indulging in a designer purchase, the experience on

Maximilianstraße is one of sophistication and elegance.

Where to Stay Nearby:
For a truly luxurious stay, consider the Hotel Vier Jahreszeiten Kempinski, located directly on Maximilianstraße. This five-star hotel offers elegant accommodations and top-tier service, making it the perfect base for a shopping spree.

Contact and Information:
- **Location:** Maximilianstraße, 80539 Munich
- **How to Get There:** Maximilianstraße is easily accessible by U-Bahn, with the Odeonsplatz and Lehel stations nearby.
- **Best Time to Visit:** Shops generally open around 10:00 AM and close by 7:00 PM. The best time to visit is during the week, when the street is less crowded.
- **Website:** www.maximilianstrasse.com (For a full list of shops and events)

2. Residenzstraße and Theatinerstraße

Just a short walk from Maximilianstraße, you'll find Residenzstraße and Theatinerstraße, two other prominent shopping streets that cater to luxury shoppers.

What to Expect:

Residenzstraße is home to high-end brands like Hermès, Cartier, and Montblanc, offering a variety of luxury goods from fashion and accessories to watches and fine pens. Theatinerstraße, on the other hand, combines luxury boutiques with upscale department stores like Kaufhaus Beck, where you can find a curated selection of designer clothing, cosmetics, and home goods.

Where to Stay Nearby:
Mandarin Oriental, Munich is an excellent choice for luxury accommodation close to both Residenzstraße and Theatinerstraße. The hotel is known for its opulent interiors and impeccable service.

Contact and Information:
- **Location:** Residenzstraße and Theatinerstraße, 80333 Munich
- **How to Get There:** Both streets are easily accessible via the Odeonsplatz U-Bahn station.
- **Best Time to Visit:** Visit during weekday afternoons for a relaxed shopping experience without the crowds.

3. Fünf Höfe

Fünf Höfe (Five Courtyards) is a modern shopping center located in the heart of Munich, offering a blend of high-end fashion, art, and gourmet food. This architecturally striking complex is known for its unique design and carefully curated selection of shops.

What to Expect:
Fünf Höfe features luxury brands such as Louis Vuitton and MCM, as well as upscale boutiques like Amorino for fine Italian fashion. The center also houses contemporary art galleries and stylish cafés, making it a destination for both shopping and culture.

Where to Stay Nearby:
Consider staying at the Platzl Hotel, located a short walk from Fünf Höfe. This boutique hotel combines traditional Bavarian style with modern comfort, offering a cozy retreat after a day of shopping.

Contact and Information:
- **Location:** Theatinerstraße 15, 80333 Munich
- **Phone:** +49 89 237070
- **Website:** www.fuenfhoefe.de
- **How to Get There:** Fünf Höfe is located near the Marienplatz and Odeonsplatz U-Bahn stations.
- **Best Time to Visit:** Fünf Höfe is best visited during the late morning or early afternoon, allowing time to explore both the shops and the art galleries.

4. Maximilianhöfe

Maximilianhöfe is another luxurious shopping destination located at the end of Maximilianstraße. This exclusive area offers a serene shopping experience away from the main thoroughfare, featuring high-end boutiques and art galleries.

What to Expect:
Maximilianhöfe is home to designer brands such as Brioni and Tod's, offering a range of luxury clothing and accessories. The complex also includes a selection of art galleries and fine dining options, making it an ideal spot for a leisurely afternoon of shopping and culture.

Where to Stay Nearby:
Hotel Bayerischer Hof, one of Munich's most prestigious hotels, is just a short distance from Maximilianhöfe. This historic hotel offers luxury accommodations and world-class amenities.

Contact and Information:
- **Location:** Maximilianstraße 13, 80539 Munich
- **Phone:** +49 89 2421780
- **Website:** www.maximilianhoefe.com
- **How to Get There:** Maximilianhöfe is best reached via the Odeonsplatz U-Bahn station.
- **Best Time to Visit:** Late afternoon is ideal for shopping, followed by a visit to one of the nearby galleries or restaurants.

B. Markets and Local Boutiques

1. Viktualienmarkt

History and Overview:
Viktualienmarkt is Munich's most famous market, with a history dating back to 1807. Originally a farmers' market, it has grown into a sprawling open-air market offering a wide variety of fresh produce, gourmet foods, and traditional Bavarian delicacies.

What to Do There:
At Viktualienmarkt, you can sample and purchase everything from fresh fruits and vegetables to exotic spices, meats, cheeses, and baked goods. Don't miss the traditional Bavarian specialties such as Weisswurst (white sausage), pretzels, and Obatzda (a cheese spread). The market also features a beer garden where you can relax with a cold brew and a hearty snack.

Where to Stay Nearby:
For a convenient stay, consider the Hotel Blauer Bock, located just a short walk from Viktualienmarkt. This boutique hotel offers a blend of modern amenities and traditional Bavarian hospitality.

Contact and Information:
- **Location:** Viktualienmarkt 3, 80331 Munich
- **Phone:** +49 89 23338960

- **Website:**
  www.muenchen.de
- **How to Get There:** Viktualienmarkt is centrally located near Marienplatz, easily accessible by U-Bahn.
- **Best Time to Visit:** The market is open Monday to Saturday from 8:00 AM to 8:00 PM. Visit in the morning for the freshest produce and a lively atmosphere.

2. Elisabethmarkt

History and Overview:
Elisabethmarkt is a smaller, lesser-known market located in the Schwabing district. Established in the late 19th century, it offers a more intimate and local shopping experience compared to the bustling Viktualienmarkt.

What to Do There:
This charming market features around 20 stalls selling a variety of goods, including fresh produce, meats, cheeses, flowers, and baked goods. It's a great place to shop for picnic supplies or to pick up unique Bavarian treats. Elisabethmarkt also has a cozy beer garden, perfect for enjoying a snack and a drink.

Where to Stay Nearby:
Stay at the Hotel la Maison, a stylish boutique hotel in Schwabing, close to Elisabethmarkt. The hotel

offers contemporary rooms and a relaxed atmosphere.

Contact and Information:
- **Location:** Elisabethplatz, 80796 Munich
- **Phone:** +49 89 23338960
- **Website:** www.muenchen.de
- **How to Get There:** Elisabethmarkt is accessible by tram, with the Elisabethplatz stop nearby.
- **Best Time to Visit:** Open Monday to Saturday from 10:00 AM to 6:00 PM. Visit around lunchtime for a quieter, more local experience.

3. Glockenbachviertel

History and Overview:
The Glockenbachviertel district is known for its trendy atmosphere and vibrant arts scene. This neighborhood is home to a variety of independent boutiques, offering everything from fashion and accessories to home decor and art.

What to Do There:
Explore the area's many boutiques, where you can find unique clothing, handmade jewelry, and art by local designers. Some popular shops include A Kind of Guise, known for its minimalist fashion, and White Rabbit's Room, which offers a curated selection of home goods and gifts. The district's

laid-back vibe makes it perfect for leisurely shopping and discovering hidden gems.

Where to Stay Nearby:
For a boutique hotel experience, consider Cortiina Hotel in the nearby Altstadt-Lehel district. It's within walking distance of Glockenbachviertel and offers stylish accommodations with a focus on comfort and design.

Contact and Information:
- **Location:** Glockenbachviertel, 80469 Munich
- **How to Get There:** The area is easily accessible by U-Bahn, with the Sendlinger Tor and Fraunhoferstraße stations nearby.
- **Best Time to Visit:** Most boutiques are open from 11:00 AM to 7:00 PM, Monday to Saturday. Weekdays are quieter, making it easier to browse at your own pace.

4. Sendlinger Straße

History and Overview:
Sendlinger Straße is one of Munich's oldest streets, located in the Altstadt (Old Town). It's a vibrant shopping destination that blends traditional Bavarian shops with modern boutiques.

What to Do There:
Along Sendlinger Straße, you'll find a mix of established brands, independent stores, and artisanal shops. Visit Lodenfrey, a historic store specializing

in traditional Bavarian clothing, or explore Tollwood, a fair-trade boutique offering sustainable fashion and gifts. The street's mix of old and new makes it a great place to shop for both classic and contemporary items.

Where to Stay Nearby:
Stay at the Hotel Mercure München Altstadt, located just a short walk from Sendlinger Straße. This hotel offers comfortable rooms and a convenient location for exploring Munich's Old Town.

Contact and Information:
- **Location:** Sendlinger Straße, 80331 Munich
- **How to Get There:** Sendlinger Straße is located near Marienplatz, easily accessible by U-Bahn.
- **Best Time to Visit:** Shops are generally open from 10:00 AM to 8:00 PM. Visit in the late morning or early afternoon to avoid the busiest times.

5. Auer Dult

History and Overview:
Auer Dult is a traditional Bavarian market held three times a year at Mariahilfplatz in the Au-Haidhausen district. Dating back over 700 years, Auer Dult is a beloved Munich tradition, offering a mix of antique goods, handmade crafts, and traditional Bavarian food.

What to Do There:
Browse the market's stalls for antiques, pottery, books, and other unique finds. The market also features food vendors selling Bavarian specialties like roast sausages, pretzels, and sweets. Auer Dult is a great place to pick up one-of-a-kind souvenirs and experience a piece of Munich's cultural heritage.

Where to Stay Nearby:
Hotel Torbräu, located near the Isartor, is a historic hotel offering comfortable accommodations with easy access to Auer Dult and other attractions.

Contact and Information:
- **Location:** Mariahilfplatz, 81541 Munich
- **Phone:** +49 89 23338960
- **Website:**
  www.auerdult.de
- **How to Get There:** Auer Dult is accessible by tram, with the Mariahilfplatz stop nearby.
- **Best Time to Visit:** Auer Dult is held in May, July, and October. The market is open from 10:00 AM to 8:00 PM, with weekends being the most popular times.

C. Souvenirs and Local Crafts

Traditional Bavarian Clothing

What to Buy:
One of the most iconic souvenirs from Munich is traditional Bavarian clothing, such as Lederhosen

for men and Dirndls for women. These garments are not only perfect for wearing to Oktoberfest but also serve as a stylish and authentic reminder of your time in Bavaria.

Where to Buy:
- **Lodenfrey:** Located on Maffeistraße, Lodenfrey is one of Munich's most famous stores for traditional Bavarian attire. Established in 1842, this historic store offers a wide selection of high-quality Lederhosen, Dirndls, and other traditional garments.
- **Angermaier Trachten:** Another excellent option is Angermaier, located on Landsberger Straße. Known for its fashionable and contemporary takes on traditional Bavarian clothing, Angermaier offers a range of options from classic designs to more modern interpretations.

Contact and Information:
- **Lodenfrey Address:** Maffeistraße 7, 80333 Munich | Phone: +49 89 210390 | Website: www.lodenfrey.com
- **Angermaier Address:** Landsberger Str. 101, 80339 Munich | Phone: +49 89 5434480 | Website: www.trachten-angermaier.de
- **Cost:** Lederhosen typically range from €150 to €500, while Dirndls can range from €100 to €400 depending on the quality and design.

- **Best Time to Visit:** Anytime during store hours, typically 10:00 AM to 7:00 PM.

Nymphenburg Porcelain

What to Buy:
Nymphenburg Porcelain is world-renowned for its exquisite craftsmanship and delicate designs. Founded in 1747, the Nymphenburg Porcelain Manufactory produces everything from elegant tableware to intricate figurines, making it a perfect souvenir for those who appreciate fine art and history.

Where to Buy:
- **Nymphenburg Porcelain Manufactory:** Located at the Nymphenburg Palace, the manufactory's showroom offers a stunning selection of handcrafted porcelain pieces. Each item is made using traditional techniques that have been passed down through generations.

Contact and Information:
- **Address:** Nördliches Schlossrondell 8, 80638 Munich
- **Phone:** +49 89 1791970
- **Website:** www.nymphenburg.com
- **Cost:** Prices vary widely, with smaller items like cups and saucers starting around €50,

and larger, more intricate pieces costing several hundred euros.

- **Best Time to Visit:** The showroom is open Monday to Saturday from 10:00 AM to 6:00 PM. Combine your visit with a tour of Nymphenburg Palace for a full cultural experience.

Handcrafted Woodwork

What to Buy:
Bavaria is famous for its handcrafted woodwork, particularly traditional carvings and toys. Items such as cuckoo clocks, Nativity scenes, and wooden toys make for charming and unique souvenirs that showcase local craftsmanship.

Where to Buy:
- **Oberpollinger:** This upscale department store on Neuhauser Straße offers a variety of handcrafted wooden items from local artisans. It's a great place to find high-quality souvenirs in a convenient central location.
- **Käthe Wohlfahrt:** Known for its Christmas decorations, Käthe Wohlfahrt also offers a selection of handcrafted wooden items, including ornaments and small decorative pieces. The store is located near Marienplatz and is a must-visit for anyone looking to bring home a piece of Bavarian tradition.

Contact and Information:

- **Oberpollinger Address:** Neuhauser Str. 18, 80331 Munich | Phone: +49 89 290210 | Website: www.oberpollinger.de
- **Käthe Wohlfahrt Address:** Weinstr. 1, 80333 Munich | Phone: +49 89 24221620 | Website: www.kaethe-wohlfahrt.com
- **Cost:** Wooden souvenirs can range from €10 for small items to €100 or more for intricate carvings or cuckoo clocks.
- **Best Time to Visit:** Visit during store hours, generally 10:00 AM to 8:00 PM.

Bavarian Beer Steins

What to Buy:
A traditional Bavarian beer stein is a classic Munich souvenir. These ceramic or pewter mugs, often decorated with ornate designs and featuring metal lids, are perfect for enjoying a beer at home or as a decorative item.

Where to Buy:
- **Hofbräuhaus Shop:** Located within the famous Hofbräuhaus beer hall, this shop offers a wide range of authentic beer steins, including ones branded with the Hofbräuhaus logo. It's a great place to pick up a souvenir after enjoying a beer in the hall.

- **Altes Hackerhaus:** Another excellent location for finding beer steins is the Altes Hackerhaus, a historic beer hall in the heart of Munich. The shop here offers a selection of traditional steins, each representing a piece of Bavarian culture.

Contact and Information:

- **Hofbräuhaus Shop Address:** Platzl 9, 80331 Munich | Phone: +49 89 2901360 | Website: www.hofbraeuhaus.de
- **Altes Hackerhaus Address:** Sendlinger Str. 14, 80331 Munich | Phone: +49 89 2605026 | Website: www.hackerhaus.de
- **Cost:** Beer steins typically range from €20 to €100, depending on the size and craftsmanship.
- **Best Time to Visit:** These shops are open during the beer hall hours, generally from late morning until late evening.

Local Delicacies

What to Buy:

If you're looking for edible souvenirs, Munich has a variety of local delicacies that make great gifts or personal treats. Items such as Lebkuchen (gingerbread), mustard, and locally brewed beer are all popular choices.

Where to Buy:

- **Dallmayr Delicatessen:** This famous gourmet store near Marienplatz offers a wide selection of high-quality local foods, including chocolates, coffee, and delicacies like Bavarian honey and mustard.
- **Viktualienmarkt:** For fresh and authentic local products, Viktualienmarkt is an excellent place to shop. Pick up some Bavarian sausages, cheese, or preserves to take home with you.

Contact and Information:

- **Dallmayr Address:** Dienerstraße 14-15, 80331 Munich | Phone: +49 89 21350 | Website: www.dallmayr.com
- **Viktualienmarkt Address:** Viktualienmarkt 3, 80331 Munich | Phone: +49 89 23338960 | Website: www.muenchen.de
- **Cost:** Prices vary depending on the product, with small edible souvenirs starting around €5.
- **Best Time to Visit:** Dallmayr is open Monday to Saturday from 9:30 AM to 7:00 PM. Viktualienmarkt is best visited in the morning for the freshest products.

D. Shopping Tips: What to Buy in Munich

1. Traditional Bavarian Souvenirs

What to Buy:
Traditional Bavarian souvenirs are a must if you want to bring home a piece of Munich's cultural heritage. Some popular items include:

- **Lederhosen and Dirndls:** These traditional garments are not only worn during Oktoberfest but are also a symbol of Bavarian pride.
- **Beer Steins:** Authentic German beer steins, often made of ceramic or pewter, are a classic souvenir that can be used or displayed as a decorative piece.
- **Cuckoo Clocks:** While originally from the Black Forest region, cuckoo clocks are a popular souvenir in Munich, showcasing intricate woodwork and craftsmanship.

Where to Buy:
- **Angermaier Trachten:** Located on Landsberger Straße, this shop offers a wide range of traditional clothing, from high-quality Lederhosen to beautifully crafted Dirndls.
- **Hofbräuhaus Shop:** For authentic beer steins, visit the shop at the famous Hofbräuhaus beer hall. They offer a variety of designs, including steins branded with the Hofbräuhaus logo.

- **Käthe Wohlfahrt:** This store near Marienplatz specializes in traditional German Christmas decorations and cuckoo clocks, making it an ideal place to find a unique, handcrafted souvenir.

2. Local Food Products

What to Buy:
Munich is famous for its food, and there are plenty of edible souvenirs you can bring home to remember your visit:

- **Lebkuchen:** A traditional Bavarian gingerbread often decorated with intricate designs, Lebkuchen is a sweet treat that makes a great gift.
- **Bavarian Mustard:** Known for its unique flavor, Bavarian mustard is a perfect accompaniment to sausages and can be found in various flavors.
- **Dallmayr Coffee:** Dallmayr is one of Munich's oldest delicatessens, and their coffee is a premium product that makes for a luxurious souvenir.

Where to Buy:
- **Viktualienmarkt:** This bustling market in the heart of Munich offers a wide selection of local food products, from fresh produce to artisanal foods. It's a great place to pick up some Bavarian mustard or Lebkuchen.
- **Dallmayr Delicatessen:** Located near Marienplatz, Dallmayr is a gourmet food

store where you can find high-quality coffee, chocolates, and other delicacies.

3. Designer and Luxury Goods

What to Buy:
If you're in the market for high-end fashion and luxury goods, Munich has plenty to offer:

- **Designer Clothing:** Munich is home to numerous luxury boutiques where you can find the latest fashion from international designers.
- **Watches and Jewelry:** German craftsmanship is world-renowned, and Munich offers a selection of fine watches and jewelry from prestigious brands.
- **Leather Goods:** Quality leather goods, including handbags, wallets, and belts, are widely available and make for a durable and stylish souvenir.

Where to Buy:
- **Maximilianstraße:** This is Munich's most famous shopping street, known for its luxury boutiques and designer stores, including Chanel, Louis Vuitton, and Gucci.
- **Fünf Höfe:** A modern shopping complex located in the city center, Fünf Höfe offers a mix of high-end fashion, art galleries, and gourmet food shops.

4. Art and Antiques

What to Buy:

Munich has a rich cultural history, and there are plenty of opportunities to purchase art and antiques that reflect the city's heritage:

- **Art Prints and Paintings:** Munich is known for its art galleries, and you can find prints or original works by local artists.
- **Antique Furniture and Decor:** From vintage Bavarian furniture to antique porcelain, Munich's antique shops offer a wide range of unique items.
- **Porcelain:** Nymphenburg Porcelain is particularly famous, known for its delicate and intricate designs.

Where to Buy:

- **Nymphenburg Porcelain Manufactory:** Located at the Nymphenburg Palace, this showroom offers a wide selection of handcrafted porcelain items.
- **Munich's Antique Shops:** Explore the areas around Maxvorstadt and Schwabing, where you'll find numerous antique shops offering everything from furniture to small decorative items.

5. Unique Boutique Finds

What to Buy:

Munich's local boutiques offer a variety of unique and handmade items that you won't find anywhere else:

- **Handmade Jewelry:** Local designers often sell their creations in small boutiques, offering unique pieces that make for a special gift or personal keepsake.
- **Fashion by Local Designers:** Munich has a vibrant fashion scene, and many local designers sell their clothing and accessories in independent boutiques.
- **Home Decor and Gifts:** From handmade candles to decorative ceramics, Munich's boutiques are full of charming items that reflect the city's style.

Where to Buy:
- **Glockenbachviertel:** This trendy neighborhood is known for its independent boutiques, where you can find everything from handmade jewelry to stylish clothing by local designers.
- **Sendlinger Straße:** A mix of traditional and modern shops, Sendlinger Straße is a great place to explore for unique gifts and souvenirs.

Shopping Tips

- **Timing:** Most shops in Munich open around 10:00 AM and close by 8:00 PM. Shops are generally closed on Sundays, so plan your shopping trips accordingly.
- **Tax-Free Shopping:** Non-EU residents can take advantage of tax-free shopping in Munich. Be sure to ask for a tax refund form

when making purchases over a certain amount, and keep your receipts to claim your refund at the airport.

- **Bargaining:** Bargaining is not common in Munich's shops, especially in high-end stores. However, it may be possible in markets or antique shops.

Chapter 9: Day Trips from Munich

A. Neuschwanstein Castle and Hohenschwangau

Neuschwanstein Castle

History and Overview:
Neuschwanstein Castle is one of the most famous castles in the world, often referred to as the "fairy-tale castle" for its romantic architecture and stunning location. Commissioned by King Ludwig II of Bavaria in 1869, Neuschwanstein was intended as a personal retreat for the king and a homage to the operas of Richard Wagner. The castle's design, with its towering turrets and ornate interiors, reflects Ludwig's love of medieval romance and his eccentric personality. Although the castle was never fully completed, it stands today as a symbol of fantasy and idealism, drawing millions of visitors each year.

What to Do There:
- **Tour the Castle:** The interior of Neuschwanstein is as impressive as its

exterior, with rooms richly decorated in themes from Wagner's operas. Highlights include the Throne Hall, with its gilded columns and Byzantine-style mosaic floor, and the King's Bedroom, adorned with elaborate wood carvings.

- **Marienbrücke (Mary's Bridge):** For the best views of Neuschwanstein, take a short walk to Marienbrücke, a bridge that spans the Pöllat Gorge. From here, you can capture the iconic image of the castle set against the backdrop of the Alps.
- **Explore the Grounds:** The area surrounding the castle is perfect for a leisurely walk or a more challenging hike, with trails offering stunning views of the Bavarian countryside.

Contact and Booking Information:
- **Address:** Neuschwansteinstraße 20, 87645 Schwangau, Germany
- **Phone:** +49 8362 930830
- **Website:** www.neuschwanstein.de
- **Cost:** Tickets for a guided tour of Neuschwanstein Castle cost approximately €15 for adults. Tickets should be booked in advance, especially during peak tourist seasons.
- **Best Time to Visit:** Neuschwanstein is beautiful year-round, but the best times to visit are in the spring and fall when the

weather is mild, and the crowds are smaller. Winter visits can also be magical, with the castle often dusted in snow.

How to Get There:
Neuschwanstein Castle is located about 120 kilometers southwest of Munich. The easiest way to reach the castle is by train or car:

- **By Train:** Take a train from Munich's Hauptbahnhof (main train station) to Füssen, which takes about 2 hours. From Füssen, a local bus will take you to the village of Hohenschwangau, where the castles are located.

- **By Car:** If you prefer to drive, the journey takes about 1.5 to 2 hours. There are parking facilities in Hohenschwangau, but be prepared for a short uphill walk to reach the castle.

Hohenschwangau Castle

History and Overview:
Hohenschwangau Castle, located just a short distance from Neuschwanstein, was the childhood home of King Ludwig II. Originally built in the 12th century, the castle was reconstructed in the 19th century by Ludwig's father, King Maximilian

II, who used it as a summer residence for the royal family. The castle's interior is filled with murals depicting Germanic legends, and it offers a more intimate and historically grounded experience compared to the grandeur of Neuschwanstein.

What to Do There:
- **Tour the Castle:** Guided tours of Hohenschwangau Castle offer insight into the daily life of the Bavarian royal family. The rooms are richly decorated with frescoes, and many of the original furnishings are still in place.
- **Visit the Gardens:** The castle's gardens are beautifully maintained and offer stunning views of the surrounding lakes and mountains.

Contact and Booking Information:
- **Address:** Alpseestraße 30, 87645 Schwangau, Germany
- **Phone:** +49 8362 930830
- **Website:** www.hohenschwangau.de
- **Cost:** Tickets for a guided tour of Hohenschwangau Castle are approximately €13 for adults. Combined tickets for both Neuschwanstein and Hohenschwangau are available at a discounted rate.
- **Best Time to Visit:** Like Neuschwanstein, Hohenschwangau is best visited in the

spring or fall for optimal weather and fewer crowds.

How to Get There:
Hohenschwangau Castle is located just a short walk from Neuschwanstein Castle. If you're visiting both, it's easy to explore Hohenschwangau first, followed by Neuschwanstein.

Planning Your Day Trip

Timing:
Plan to spend a full day visiting Neuschwanstein and Hohenschwangau. Start your day early to avoid the crowds, especially during the summer months. Allow time for the guided tours, a walk to Marienbrücke, and a leisurely lunch in the village of Hohenschwangau.

Where to Eat:
There are several restaurants and cafés in Hohenschwangau village where you can enjoy traditional Bavarian cuisine. Alpenrose am See is a popular choice, offering stunning views of the Alpsee lake along with a menu of regional dishes.

Accessibility:
Both castles require some walking, and Neuschwanstein in particular involves a steep climb. Shuttle buses and horse-drawn carriages are available for those who prefer not to walk.

Souvenirs:

Don't forget to visit the gift shops at both castles, where you can purchase souvenirs such as postcards, books, and small replicas of the castles.

B. Dachau Concentration Camp Memorial

History and Overview

Dachau Concentration Camp was opened on March 22, 1933, shortly after Adolf Hitler became Chancellor of Germany. Initially intended for political prisoners, Dachau quickly expanded to imprison Jews, Roma, disabled individuals, and others deemed undesirable by the Nazi regime. Over the twelve years of its operation, more than 200,000 prisoners were held at Dachau, with tens of thousands dying due to the brutal conditions, forced labor, medical experiments, and executions.

After the camp was liberated by American forces on April 29, 1945, Dachau became a symbol of the atrocities committed during the Holocaust. In 1965, the site was established as a memorial, ensuring that the horrors of the past would never be forgotten.

What to Do There

- **Visit the Memorial Museum:** The Dachau Memorial Museum offers a comprehensive and deeply affecting look at the history of the camp. The museum's exhibits include photographs, documents, and artifacts that detail the lives of the prisoners, the conditions they endured, and the history of the Nazi regime. The museum also features a 22-minute documentary film that provides an overview of the camp's history and its role in the Holocaust.

- **Tour the Camp Grounds:** The grounds of the Dachau Memorial include several preserved and reconstructed buildings, such as the prisoner barracks, the crematorium, and the administration buildings. Walking through these areas, you can gain a visceral understanding of the scale and brutality of the camp. The reconstructed barracks provide insight into the overcrowded and inhumane living conditions faced by prisoners, while the crematorium complex serves as a stark reminder of the camp's deadly purpose.

- **Reflect at the Religious Memorials:** The site includes several religious memorials, such as the Jewish Memorial, the Catholic Mortal Agony of Christ Chapel, and the Protestant Church of Reconciliation. These places of worship offer a quiet space for reflection and prayer, serving as a reminder of the spiritual resilience of those who suffered and died at Dachau.

- **Walk the Path of Remembrance:** The Path of Remembrance is a route that takes you through significant locations around the camp, including the roll-call square and the perimeter fence. This walk provides a deeper understanding of the daily life and suffering endured by the prisoners.

Contact and Booking Information:

- **Address:** Alte Römerstraße 75, 85221 Dachau, Germany
- **Phone:** +49 8131 669970
- **Website:** www.kz-gedenkstaette-dachau.de
- **Cost:** Admission to the Dachau Memorial Site is free, but donations are encouraged. Guided tours are available for a fee, typically around €4 per person. Audio guides are also available for a small fee.
- **Best Time to Visit:** The memorial is open year-round, but it is best visited during the spring or fall for milder weather. The site is open daily from 9:00 AM to 5:00 PM, except on December 24th.

How to Get There:

Dachau is located about 16 kilometers northwest of Munich and is easily accessible by public transportation:

- **By Train:** Take the S2 S-Bahn line from Munich's Hauptbahnhof (main train station) to Dachau station, which takes about 25 minutes. From the Dachau station, you can take bus 726 directly to the memorial site.
- **By Car:** If you prefer to drive, the journey from Munich takes about 30 minutes. There is parking available at the memorial site for a small fee.

Planning Your Visit

Timing:
A visit to the Dachau Memorial typically takes about 3 to 4 hours, depending on how much time you spend at each exhibit and whether you take a guided tour. It's recommended to start your visit in the morning to avoid crowds and allow enough time for reflection.

Where to Eat:
There is a small café on the grounds of the memorial that offers light refreshments and snacks. Alternatively, the town of Dachau has several restaurants and cafés where you can enjoy a meal before or after your visit.

What to Bring:
Comfortable walking shoes are essential, as much of the site is outdoors, and you'll be walking on

gravel paths. It's also advisable to bring water, especially if you're visiting during the warmer months. Remember to dress respectfully, as this is a place of remembrance.

Guided Tours:
To gain a deeper understanding of the history and significance of Dachau, consider joining one of the guided tours offered at the memorial. These tours are led by knowledgeable guides who provide detailed information and context, enhancing the educational aspect of your visit.

C. Salzburg, Austria

Getting to Salzburg

By Train:
The easiest and most convenient way to reach Salzburg from Munich is by train. The journey takes approximately 1.5 to 2 hours, with regular departures from Munich's Hauptbahnhof (main train station). You can purchase a Bayern-Ticket, which offers unlimited travel for a day within Bavaria and to Salzburg, making it an economical option for groups or solo travelers. The

Bayern-Ticket also covers local public transportation within Salzburg.

By Car:
If you prefer driving, the journey from Munich to Salzburg takes about 1.5 hours via the A8 motorway. Be sure to have a vignette (toll sticker) if you plan to drive on Austrian highways. Parking can be found in the city center, but it's recommended to park slightly outside the city and use public transport to explore.

By Bus:
FlixBus and other bus services offer affordable and comfortable rides from Munich to Salzburg, with travel times ranging from 2 to 2.5 hours. This can be a cost-effective option, especially if you book in advance.

What to See and Do in Salzburg

1. Explore the Old Town (Altstadt):
Salzburg's Old Town is a UNESCO World Heritage Site, famous for its well-preserved Baroque architecture and charming narrow streets. Begin your exploration at the Salzburg Cathedral, a stunning example of Baroque architecture with its twin towers and impressive dome. Nearby, the Residenzplatz and Mozartplatz squares are perfect for strolling and taking in the historical atmosphere.

2. Visit Mozart's Birthplace:

Mozart's Birthplace (Mozart Geburtshaus) is one of Salzburg's most famous attractions. Located on Getreidegasse, a bustling shopping street, this museum offers a fascinating look into the life and work of Wolfgang Amadeus Mozart. The museum displays original instruments, letters, and personal items belonging to the composer, providing insight into his early life and career.

3. Hohensalzburg Fortress:
Perched atop the Festungsberg hill, the Hohensalzburg Fortress is one of the largest and best-preserved medieval castles in Europe. You can reach the fortress by foot or by taking a funicular from the Old Town. The fortress offers stunning panoramic views of Salzburg and the surrounding Alps, as well as exhibitions on the history of the castle and Salzburg itself. Don't miss the Fortress Museum and the Marionette Museum, which add cultural depth to your visit.

4. Mirabell Palace and Gardens:
Mirabell Palace and its beautiful gardens are a must-see in Salzburg. The palace was originally built in 1606 and is now home to the city's municipal offices, but the real highlight is the meticulously maintained gardens. The Mirabell Gardens are famous for their floral patterns, fountains, and sculptures, and were featured in the iconic "Do-Re-Mi" scene from The Sound of Music. It's a perfect spot for a leisurely walk and some photo opportunities.

5. St. Peter's Abbey and Cemetery:

Located at the foot of the Mönchsberg, St. Peter's Abbey is one of the oldest monasteries in the German-speaking world, founded in 696 AD. The abbey church is a beautiful example of Romanesque and Baroque architecture. Adjacent to the abbey is St. Peter's Cemetery, one of the most picturesque cemeteries in Europe, with ornate tombs and chapels. The cemetery is also where some scenes from The Sound of Music were filmed.

6. Take a River Cruise on the Salzach:

For a different perspective of the city, consider taking a boat cruise on the Salzach River. The cruises offer a relaxing way to see Salzburg's landmarks from the water, with views of the Old Town, the fortress, and the surrounding mountains. Some cruises also include dinner and live music, adding a special touch to your visit.

Where to Eat and Drink

Salzburg offers a variety of dining options, from traditional Austrian cuisine to international fare. Here are a few recommendations:

- **St. Peter Stiftskeller:** Known as the oldest restaurant in Central Europe, dating back to 803 AD, St. Peter Stiftskeller offers an elegant dining experience with traditional Austrian dishes such as Wiener Schnitzel and Tafelspitz (boiled beef).

- **Café Tomaselli:** A historic café that has been serving coffee since 1705, Café Tomaselli is the perfect place to enjoy a slice of Sachertorte (chocolate cake) or an Apfelstrudel (apple strudel) with a cup of coffee.
- **Augustiner Bräustübl:** If you're in the mood for a beer, head to the Augustiner Bräustübl, a traditional brewery and beer hall where you can enjoy freshly brewed beer in a lively and historic setting.

Shopping in Salzburg

Salzburg's Old Town is home to a variety of shops and boutiques, where you can find everything from Mozartkugeln (chocolate pralines filled with marzipan and nougat) to high-end fashion. Getreidegasse is the main shopping street, offering a mix of traditional Austrian crafts, souvenirs, and international brands.

Practical Information

- **Language:** German is the official language, but English is widely spoken in tourist areas.
- **Currency:** The Euro (€) is the currency used in Austria. Credit cards are widely accepted, but it's a good idea to carry some cash for smaller purchases.
- **Time Zone:** Salzburg operates on Central European Time (CET).

- **Weather:** Salzburg has a temperate climate with distinct seasons. Summers are warm and pleasant, making it ideal for outdoor exploration, while winters can be cold and snowy, adding a magical touch to the city's scenery.

Best Time to Visit

Salzburg is beautiful year-round, but the best time to visit is during the spring (April to June) and fall (September to October) when the weather is mild, and the city is less crowded. If you're a fan of Christmas markets, visiting in December is also a great option, as Salzburg's Christmas markets are some of the most festive in Europe.

D. The Bavarian Alps

Hiking in the Bavarian Alps

Where to Go:
- **Garmisch-Partenkirchen:** One of the most popular destinations for hiking, Garmisch-Partenkirchen is about 90 minutes from Munich by car or train. This charming town is surrounded by trails that cater to all

levels of hikers. For an easy hike, explore the Partnach Gorge (Partnachklamm), a spectacular ravine with a walkway carved into the rock, offering breathtaking views of the rushing waters below. For a more challenging hike, consider the trail up to the Alpspitze, a peak that offers panoramic views of the surrounding mountains and valleys.

- **Tegernsee:** Located about an hour from Munich, Tegernsee is a beautiful lake surrounded by mountains, with numerous hiking trails that offer stunning views of the water and the alpine landscape. The hike to the Wallberg summit is particularly popular, offering a moderate challenge with rewarding views at the top. After your hike, you can relax by the lake or enjoy a meal at one of the traditional Bavarian restaurants in the area.

- **Berchtesgaden National Park:** For those seeking a more remote and untouched natural setting, Berchtesgaden National Park is about two hours from Munich and offers some of the most dramatic scenery in the Bavarian Alps. The Königssee lake, with its emerald waters and steep mountain cliffs, is a highlight, as is the hike to the Watzmann massif, the third-highest peak in Germany. This area is perfect for experienced hikers looking for more challenging trails.

What to Bring:

- **Hiking Boots:** Sturdy, comfortable hiking boots are essential for navigating the often rugged terrain of the Alps.
- **Weather-Appropriate Clothing:** The weather in the mountains can change rapidly, so it's important to dress in layers and bring a waterproof jacket.
- **Backpack:** A small backpack with water, snacks, a map, and a first-aid kit is recommended for any hike.

Best Time to Visit:
The best time for hiking in the Bavarian Alps is from late spring to early autumn (May to October), when the trails are clear of snow and the weather is mild. July and August are the busiest months, so consider visiting in June or September for fewer crowds.

Skiing in the Bavarian Alps

Where to Go:

- **Garmisch-Partenkirchen (Garmisch Classic and Zugspitze):** Garmisch-Partenkirchen is not only a hiking destination but also home to some of the best skiing in Germany. The Garmisch Classic area offers a variety of slopes suitable for all skill levels, while the Zugspitze glacier, Germany's highest peak, offers skiing year-round. The Zugspitze ski area provides reliable snow and stunning views, making it a top choice for skiers and snowboarders alike.

- **Oberstdorf:** Located about two hours from Munich, Oberstdorf is another excellent skiing destination, offering over 130 kilometers of slopes in the Fellhorn-Kanzelwand ski area. This resort is known for its well-groomed slopes, modern lifts, and a variety of terrain that caters to beginners, intermediates, and advanced skiers. The Nebelhorn mountain in Oberstdorf also offers challenging runs and breathtaking alpine scenery.

- **Berchtesgaden:** For a more relaxed and family-friendly skiing experience, Berchtesgaden offers several smaller ski areas, such as Jenner and Götschen, which are perfect for beginners and those looking for a quieter atmosphere. The area also offers opportunities for cross-country skiing and snowshoeing.

What to Bring:
- **Ski Gear:** If you don't have your own ski gear, you can rent equipment at most ski resorts. Be sure to dress warmly with thermal layers, a waterproof jacket, and gloves.

- **Lift Pass:** Lift passes can usually be purchased on-site or online in advance, often with discounts for multi-day passes.
- **Sunscreen and Goggles:** The sun's reflection off the snow can be intense, so bring sunscreen and ski goggles to protect your skin and eyes.

Best Time to Visit:

The skiing season in the Bavarian Alps typically runs from December to April, with the best snow conditions usually found in January and February. Early season (December) and late season (March to April) can offer fewer crowds and lower prices, but snow conditions can be more variable.

Planning Your Day Trip

Getting There:

- **By Train:** The Bavarian Alps are easily accessible from Munich by train, with regular services to Garmisch-Partenkirchen, Tegernsee, Oberstdorf, and Berchtesgaden. The Bayern-Ticket is a convenient and cost-effective option for unlimited travel within Bavaria.
- **By Car:** Driving offers flexibility, especially if you plan to visit multiple locations in one day. The A95 and A8 highways are the main routes from Munich to the Alps, and parking is usually available at ski resorts and trailheads.

Where to Eat:

- **Mountain Huts (Almhütten):** During your hike or ski trip, stop at one of the many mountain huts (Almhütten) that dot the trails and slopes. These cozy, rustic establishments serve hearty Bavarian fare such as Kaiserschmarrn (shredded pancakes), Wiener Schnitzel, and local sausages, along with warm drinks like hot chocolate or mulled wine.
- **Local Restaurants:** After a day of outdoor activity, enjoy a meal at a traditional Bavarian restaurant in one of the alpine towns. Look for dishes like Schweinshaxe (pork knuckle) and Knödel (dumplings), and don't forget to try a locally brewed beer.

What to Do Afterward:

After your hike or ski session, unwind in one of the local spa facilities or thermal baths available in towns like Garmisch-Partenkirchen or Tegernsee. Many of these spas offer panoramic views of the mountains, providing the perfect way to relax and rejuvenate after a day of adventure.

E. Lakes and Countryside Retreats

1. Lake Tegernsee

Overview:

Lake Tegernsee, located about an hour south of Munich, is one of Bavaria's most beautiful and popular lakes. Surrounded by the Bavarian Alps, Tegernsee offers stunning views, clear waters, and a variety of outdoor activities. The lake is known for its clean, swimmable waters and the charming town of Tegernsee on its shores.

What to Do There:

- **Boat Rides:** Take a leisurely boat ride across the lake to enjoy the stunning scenery. Boat tours are available throughout the day and offer a relaxing way to see the surrounding mountains and villages.
- **Hiking and Biking:** There are numerous hiking and biking trails around Lake Tegernsee, ranging from easy walks along the shoreline to more challenging mountain hikes. The hike to the summit of the Wallberg is particularly rewarding, offering panoramic views of the lake and the Alps.
- **Visit Tegernsee Town:** The town of Tegernsee is home to the historic Tegernsee Abbey, a former Benedictine monastery now housing a brewery and a restaurant. Enjoy a traditional Bavarian meal at the Bräustüberl Tegernsee, and don't forget to try their famous beer.

Contact and Information:

- **Location:** Lake Tegernsee, 83700 Tegernsee, Germany
- **How to Get There:** Tegernsee is easily accessible by train from Munich's Hauptbahnhof. The journey takes about an hour, and the train station is a short walk from the lake.
- **Best Time to Visit:** Summer is the best time to visit Tegernsee for swimming and boating, while autumn offers beautiful foliage and quieter trails.

2. Lake Starnberg

Overview:

Lake Starnberg, just 25 kilometers southwest of Munich, is a favorite retreat for both locals and visitors. Known as one of the largest and cleanest lakes in Bavaria, Starnberg is surrounded by elegant villas, lush parks, and scenic paths, making it an ideal destination for a relaxing day trip.

What to Do There:

- **Swimming and Sunbathing:** The lake's clear waters are perfect for swimming, and there are several designated swimming areas and beaches around the lake. Strandbad Starnberg is one of the most popular spots, offering a sandy beach, sunbathing lawns, and facilities for families.
- **Boat Excursions:** Take a boat cruise around Lake Starnberg to enjoy the peaceful atmosphere and scenic beauty. The cruise

offers views of the lakeside mansions, wooded hills, and distant Alps.

- **Explore the Villages:** Visit the picturesque villages of Tutzing or Possenhofen, where you can stroll along the lakeshore, visit local cafés, and learn about the lake's connection to Bavarian royalty. Possenhofen is famous for its association with Empress Elisabeth of Austria (Sisi), who spent her childhood at Possenhofen Castle.

Contact and Information:
- **Location:** Lake Starnberg, 82319 Starnberg, Germany
- **How to Get There:** Lake Starnberg is easily reached by the S6 S-Bahn line from Munich, with the journey taking about 30 minutes. The Starnberg station is located right by the lake.
- **Best Time to Visit:** Summer is ideal for swimming and boating, while spring and autumn offer pleasant weather for walking and exploring the villages.

3. Lake Chiemsee

Overview:

Lake Chiemsee, often referred to as the "Bavarian Sea," is the largest lake in Bavaria and one of the most popular destinations in the region. Located about an hour and a half east of Munich, Chiemsee is known for its crystal-clear waters, beautiful islands, and the majestic Herrenchiemsee Palace.

What to Do There:

- **Visit Herrenchiemsee Palace:** One of the main attractions at Lake Chiemsee is Herrenchiemsee Palace, built by King Ludwig II as a tribute to the Palace of Versailles. The palace is located on Herreninsel (Men's Island) and is accessible by boat. Tour the opulent rooms, including the Hall of Mirrors, and explore the beautiful gardens surrounding the palace.
- **Explore Fraueninsel:** Another highlight of Lake Chiemsee is Fraueninsel (Women's Island), home to a Benedictine convent and a picturesque village. The island is car-free, making it a peaceful place to walk, visit artisan shops, and enjoy fresh fish from the lake.
- **Water Sports and Swimming:** Lake Chiemsee offers excellent opportunities for water sports, including sailing, windsurfing, and paddleboarding. There are also several beaches where you can swim or relax by the water.

Contact and Information:

- **Location:** Lake Chiemsee, 83256 Prien am Chiemsee, Germany
- **How to Get There:** Take a train from Munich to Prien am Chiemsee, which takes about 1.5 hours. From Prien, boats depart regularly to the islands.

- **Best Time to Visit:** Summer is the best time for water activities and exploring the islands. The lake is also beautiful in the spring and fall, with fewer tourists and milder weather.

4. Lake Ammersee

Overview:
Lake Ammersee, located about 35 kilometers southwest of Munich, is a peaceful retreat known for its tranquil waters and idyllic countryside. The lake is less crowded than some of the other Bavarian lakes, making it an ideal destination for those seeking relaxation and natural beauty.

What to Do There:
- **Boat Trips:** Enjoy a leisurely boat trip around Lake Ammersee, with stops at charming lakeside villages such as Herrsching and Dießen. The boat rides offer stunning views of the Alps and the lush green landscape surrounding the lake.
- **Kloster Andechs:** One of the highlights near Lake Ammersee is Kloster Andechs, a Benedictine monastery famous for its brewery and beer garden. After a hike up to the monastery, reward yourself with a cold beer and traditional Bavarian food while enjoying panoramic views of the countryside.
- **Swimming and Relaxing:** Lake Ammersee has several quiet spots where you can swim,

sunbathe, or simply relax by the water. Herrsching, in particular, has a lovely lakeside promenade and a designated swimming area.

Contact and Information:

- **Location:** Lake Ammersee, 82211 Herrsching am Ammersee, Germany
- **How to Get There:** Lake Ammersee is accessible by the S8 S-Bahn line from Munich, with the journey taking about 45 minutes. The Herrsching station is close to the lake.
- **Best Time to Visit:** Summer is perfect for swimming and boating, while autumn offers beautiful foliage and fewer crowds.

Planning Your Day Trip

Timing:

Plan to spend a full day at any of these lakes or countryside retreats. Start your day early to make the most of your time, especially if you plan to visit multiple locations or take a boat trip.

Where to Eat:

Bavaria's lakeside villages are home to many traditional restaurants and beer gardens where you can enjoy hearty Bavarian cuisine. Freshly caught fish from the lakes is a local specialty, often served with potatoes and salad. Be sure to try local desserts like Kaiserschmarrn (shredded pancakes) or Apfelstrudel (apple strudel).

What to Bring:
- **Comfortable Clothing:** Wear comfortable clothing suitable for walking or light hiking, and bring a swimsuit if you plan to swim.
- **Sunscreen and Hat:** Protect yourself from the sun, especially if you'll be spending a lot of time outdoors.
- **Camera:** The stunning landscapes around Bavaria's lakes provide endless photo opportunities.

Weather Considerations:
Weather in the Bavarian countryside can be changeable, so it's wise to check the forecast before your trip and be prepared for varying conditions, especially if you're visiting in spring or autumn.

Chapter 10: Munich Nightlife and Entertainment

A. Best Bars and Pubs

Hofbräuhaus München

Overview:
No visit to Munich is complete without a stop at the Hofbräuhaus, one of the city's most famous beer halls. Established in 1589, Hofbräuhaus has become a symbol of Bavarian culture, offering a lively atmosphere, traditional Bavarian music, and, of course, great beer. The beer hall is spread over several floors, including a large beer garden, making it a perfect spot to experience the conviviality of Munich's pub culture.

What to Drink:
Hofbräuhaus serves its own brews, including the classic Hofbräu Original, a full-bodied lager, and

Hofbräu Dunkel, a dark beer with rich, malty flavors. Be sure to order a Maß, the traditional one-liter beer stein, and pair it with a hearty Bavarian pretzel or a plate of Weisswurst.

Contact and Information:

- **Address:** Platzl 9, 80331 Munich
- **Phone:** +49 89 2901360
- **Website:** www.hofbraeuhaus.de
- **Opening Hours:** Daily from 9:00 AM to midnight
- **Atmosphere:** Lively and historic, with live traditional Bavarian music in the evenings

Augustiner Keller

Overview:

Augustiner Keller is another iconic Munich beer hall, known for its authentic Bavarian atmosphere and large beer garden. Founded in 1812, it's one of the oldest beer halls in the city and is beloved by locals for its traditional setting and excellent beer. The beer garden, shaded by chestnut trees, is particularly popular in the warmer months.

What to Drink:

Augustiner Keller serves beer from the Augustiner Brewery, Munich's oldest privately-owned brewery. The Augustiner Helles, a smooth, golden lager, is a favorite among regulars. If you're visiting in the fall, be sure to try the Augustiner Oktoberfestbier.

Contact and Information:
- **Address:** Arnulfstraße 52, 80335 Munich
- **Phone:** +49 89 594393
- **Website:** www.augustinerkeller.de
- **Opening Hours:** Daily from 10:00 AM to midnight
- **Atmosphere:** Traditional and relaxed, with a spacious beer garden that's perfect for socializing

Schumann's Bar

Overview:
For a more upscale and sophisticated drinking experience, Schumann's Bar is the place to go. Located on the Odeonsplatz, this legendary cocktail bar has been a staple of Munich's nightlife since 1982. Founded by Charles Schumann, a renowned bartender and author, the bar is known for its expertly crafted cocktails and elegant atmosphere.

What to Drink:
Schumann's Bar offers a wide selection of classic cocktails, including the Negroni, Martini, and Old Fashioned, all made with premium spirits and impeccable attention to detail. The bar's extensive whiskey collection is also worth exploring.

Contact and Information:
- **Address:** Odeonsplatz 6+7, 80539 Munich

- **Phone:** +49 89 229060
- **Website:**
  www.schumanns.de
- **Opening Hours:** Monday to Saturday, 12:00 PM to 3:00 AM; closed on Sundays
- **Atmosphere:** Sophisticated and stylish, with a focus on quality and service

Zum Wolf

Overview:
Zum Wolf is a cozy, dimly-lit bar located in the trendy Glockenbachviertel district. Known for its laid-back vibe and excellent selection of drinks, Zum Wolf is a favorite among locals and visitors alike. The bar features a vintage-inspired interior with wooden furnishings, creating a warm and inviting atmosphere.

What to Drink:
The bar specializes in craft cocktails, with a menu that changes regularly based on seasonal ingredients. Try one of their signature creations, or ask the knowledgeable bartenders for a recommendation. Zum Wolf also offers a good selection of local and international beers, as well as a variety of wines.

Contact and Information:
- **Address:** Pestalozzistraße 22, 80469 Munich
- **Phone:** +49 89 20106542

- **Website:** No official website; find them on social media for updates
- **Opening Hours:** Daily from 7:00 PM to 2:00 AM
- **Atmosphere:** Intimate and relaxed, with a focus on craft cocktails and good conversation

The Flushing Meadows Bar

Overview:
Located on the rooftop of The Flushing Meadows Hotel, this bar offers stunning views of Munich's skyline along with creative cocktails. The bar's modern design and chic atmosphere make it a popular spot for both locals and tourists, especially during the warmer months when the outdoor terrace is open.

What to Drink:
The cocktail menu at The Flushing Meadows Bar is inventive, featuring both classic and contemporary creations. The bar's signature cocktails often incorporate fresh herbs and unusual ingredients, providing a unique drinking experience. The "Munich Mule," a local twist on the Moscow Mule, is a must-try.

Contact and Information:
- **Address:** Fraunhoferstraße 32, 80469 Munich
- **Phone:** +49 89 55279170

- **Website:**
  www.flushingmeadowshotel.com
- **Opening Hours:** Wednesday to Saturday, 6:00 PM to 2:00 AM
- **Atmosphere:** Modern and trendy, with a focus on creative cocktails and panoramic views

Giesinger Bräu

Overview:

For a more local and authentic experience, visit Giesinger Bräu, a small independent brewery and pub in the Giesing district. This microbrewery has gained a loyal following for its handcrafted beers and unpretentious atmosphere. The pub is a great place to enjoy fresh, unfiltered beer brewed on-site.

What to Drink:

Giesinger Bräu offers a variety of beers, including traditional lagers, wheat beers, and seasonal brews. The Giesinger Erhellung, a light, refreshing lager, is a local favorite. Be sure to try one of their limited-edition brews if available.

Contact and Information:

- **Address:** Martin-Luther-Straße 2, 81539 Munich
- **Phone:** +49 89 45145155
- **Website:**
  www.giesinger-braeu.de

- **Opening Hours:** Monday to Thursday, 4:00 PM to 10:00 PM; Friday to Sunday, 11:00 AM to 11:00 PM
- **Atmosphere:** Casual and friendly, with a focus on local craft beer and community

B. Theatres and Cultural Performances

1. National Theatre (Nationaltheater)

Overview:
The National Theatre in Munich is home to the Bavarian State Opera and the Bavarian State Ballet, making it one of the most prestigious cultural institutions in Germany. Located in the heart of the city on Max-Joseph-Platz, this historic theatre is renowned for its world-class productions of opera, ballet, and classical concerts. The building itself is a stunning example of neoclassical architecture, adding to the grandeur of any evening spent here.

What to Expect:
Attending a performance at the National Theatre is a truly memorable experience. The Bavarian State Opera is known for its high-quality productions, featuring some of the best singers, conductors, and musicians in the world. The repertoire includes classic operas by composers such as Mozart, Verdi, and Wagner, as well as contemporary works. The ballet performances are equally impressive, with a focus on both classical and modern choreography. Be sure to check the theatre's schedule ahead of

time to book tickets for a performance that interests you.

Contact and Information:
- **Address:** Max-Joseph-Platz 2, 80539 Munich
- **Phone:** +49 89 218501
- **Website:** www.staatsoper.de
- **Atmosphere:** Elegant and sophisticated, perfect for a night of high culture.

2. Residenz Theatre (Residenztheater)

Overview:
The Residenz Theatre, also known as the Cuvilliés Theatre, is one of Munich's most beautiful and historic venues. Originally built in 1753, this Rococo-style theatre was destroyed during World War II but was meticulously rebuilt to its former glory. The theatre is part of the Munich Residenz complex, which was once the royal palace of the Bavarian monarchs. Today, it is home to the Bavarian State Theatre, which presents a diverse program of plays, classical works, and contemporary dramas.

What to Expect:
The Residenz Theatre offers a more intimate setting compared to larger venues, allowing for a closer connection with the performances. The theatre's repertoire includes everything from classic German

plays to modern international works, often featuring renowned actors and directors. The lavish interior, with its ornate decorations and red velvet seats, adds to the experience, making any performance here feel like a special occasion.

Contact and Information:
- **Address:** Residenzstraße 1, 80333 Munich
- **Phone:** +49 89 21851920
- **Website:** www.residenztheater.de
- **Atmosphere:** Historic and intimate, with a focus on classic and contemporary theatre.

3. Gärtnerplatz Theatre (Staatstheater am Gärtnerplatz)

Overview:
The Gärtnerplatz Theatre is Munich's leading venue for operettas, musicals, and dance performances. Located in the vibrant Gärtnerplatzviertel district, this theatre offers a more casual and lively atmosphere compared to the grander opera houses. The theatre's diverse program includes everything from light-hearted musicals to contemporary dance performances, making it a popular choice for those looking for something different.

What to Expect:
The Gärtnerplatz Theatre is known for its accessible and entertaining productions, appealing to a broad audience. Whether you're watching a classic

operetta, a popular musical, or a modern dance show, you can expect high-quality performances and engaging storytelling. The theatre also hosts concerts and special events, adding to its eclectic repertoire. The lively neighborhood around the theatre offers plenty of options for pre-show dining or post-show drinks.

Contact and Information:
- **Address:** Gärtnerplatz 3, 80469 Munich
- **Phone:** +49 89 21851960
- **Website:** www.gaertnerplatztheater.de
- **Opening Hours:** Performance times vary; check the website for the current schedule.
- **Atmosphere:** Casual and fun, with a focus on musicals, operettas, and dance.

4. Munich Kammerspiele

Overview:
The Munich Kammerspiele is one of the most important theatres in Germany for contemporary drama and experimental theatre. Founded in 1911, the Kammerspiele is known for its innovative productions and cutting-edge performances. The theatre regularly collaborates with international playwrights, directors, and artists, making it a hub for new ideas and creative expression. The Kammerspiele is located in the city center, near the Isartor, and consists of several stages, including the historic Schauspielhaus.

What to Expect:

If you're interested in thought-provoking theatre that pushes boundaries, the Munich Kammerspiele is the place to go. The theatre's program includes a mix of new plays, modern adaptations of classic works, and avant-garde performances. The productions often address contemporary social and political issues, making for an intellectually stimulating experience. The audience at the Kammerspiele is typically younger and more diverse, reflecting the theatre's commitment to innovation and inclusivity.

Contact and Information:

- **Address:** Maximilianstraße 26-28, 80539 Munich
- **Phone:** +49 89 23396600
- **Website:** www.muenchner-kammerspiele.de
- **Atmosphere:** Modern and experimental, with a focus on contemporary drama and innovative performances.

5. Prinzregententheater

Overview:

The Prinzregententheater is a stunning example of Art Nouveau architecture and is one of Munich's most beloved cultural venues. Originally opened in 1901, the theatre has been beautifully restored and now hosts a wide range of performances, including opera, classical concerts, and theatre. The theatre is located in the Bogenhausen district and offers a more intimate alternative to the larger National Theatre.

What to Expect:
The Prinzregententheater offers a diverse program that includes both classical and contemporary performances. The theatre is particularly known for its excellent acoustics, making it a popular venue for concerts and operas. The beautifully decorated interior, with its elegant balconies and chandeliers, adds to the sense of occasion when attending a performance here. The theatre also offers guided tours, giving visitors a chance to learn more about its history and architecture.

Contact and Information:
- **Address:** Prinzregentenplatz 12, 81675 Munich
- **Phone:** +49 89 218502
- **Website:** www.prinzregententheater.de
- **Opening Hours:** Performance times vary; check the website for the current schedule.
- **Atmosphere:** Elegant and historic, with a focus on opera, classical music, and theatre.

C. Cinemas and Alternative Nightlife

Independent and Art-House Cinemas

Munich has a rich tradition of cinema, with several independent and art-house theaters that showcase everything from classic films to contemporary independent cinema. These venues offer a more intimate and curated film experience, often in historic or unique settings.

1. Cinema München

Overview:
Cinema München is one of the most beloved independent cinemas in the city, known for screening a mix of international films, art-house movies, and original-language films. Located in the city center, near Stachus, this small cinema has a cozy, retro atmosphere that's perfect for a relaxed evening out. The theater often hosts special events, such as film festivals, director Q&A sessions, and themed movie nights.

What to Expect:
Cinema München is particularly popular for its screenings of films in their original language, often with German subtitles. The cinema's program is diverse, featuring everything from indie gems and documentaries to cult classics. The seating is comfortable, and the intimate setting allows for a more personal movie-going experience.

Contact and Information:
- **Address:** Nymphenburger Str. 31, 80335 Munich
- **Phone:** +49 89 555255

- **Website:**
  [www.cinema-muenchen.de](https://www.ci nema-muenchen.de)
- **Atmosphere:** Cozy and retro, with a focus on independent and international cinema.

2. Neues Arena

Overview:
Neues Arena is another iconic art-house cinema in Munich, located in the vibrant Glockenbachviertel district. This cinema is known for its eclectic selection of films, including European cinema, documentaries, and independent productions. The small, intimate theater is a favorite among film lovers who appreciate a more alternative and thought-provoking film selection.

What to Expect:
Neues Arena offers a unique cinematic experience, with a program that often includes lesser-known films and works by emerging filmmakers. The cinema's intimate size and relaxed atmosphere make it a great place to discover new films or enjoy a more low-key night out. The surrounding neighborhood is full of bars and restaurants, making it easy to combine your movie night with a drink or dinner.

Contact and Information:
- **Address:** Hans-Sachs-Straße 7, 80469 Munich
- **Phone:** +49 89 2603265

- **Website:**
  [www.neuesarena.de](https://www.neuesare
  na.de)
- **Atmosphere:** Intimate and eclectic, with a
  focus on European and independent cinema.

3. Museum Lichtspiele

Overview:
Museum Lichtspiele is one of Munich's oldest
cinemas, having opened its doors in 1910. This
historic venue has retained much of its old-world
charm, with vintage decor and a unique ambiance.
The cinema is known for its diverse program, which
includes everything from mainstream films to indie
releases, as well as regular screenings of cult
classics like The Rocky Horror Picture Show.

What to Expect:
Visiting Museum Lichtspiele is like stepping back
in time, with its classic red velvet seats and vintage
posters adorning the walls. The cinema's program is
varied, offering something for everyone, whether
you're in the mood for a new release or a beloved
classic. The regular midnight screenings of The
Rocky Horror Picture Show are a particular
highlight, complete with audience participation and
costumes.

Contact and Information:
- **Address:** Lilienstraße 2, 81669 Munich
- **Phone:** +49 89 4486996

- **Website:**
  www.museum-lichtspiele.de
- **Atmosphere:** Historic and nostalgic, with a diverse film selection.

D. Alternative Nightlife Venues

1. Substanz

Overview:
Substanz is a popular alternative venue in Munich that combines a bar, club, and live performance space. Located in the Ludwigsvorstadt-Isarvorstadt district, Substanz has a laid-back, underground vibe and hosts a wide range of events, including live music, stand-up comedy, poetry slams, and DJ nights. The venue's diverse program and unpretentious atmosphere make it a favorite among those looking for an alternative night out.

What to Expect:
Substanz offers something different every night, from local bands and comedy shows to themed DJ nights. The venue has a relaxed, intimate feel, with a mix of seating areas and a small dance floor. The drinks menu includes a variety of beers, cocktails, and non-alcoholic options, all reasonably priced. Substanz is a great place to catch live performances in a more casual setting or to enjoy a night of dancing without the typical club scene.

Contact and Information:

- **Address:** Ruppertstraße 28, 80337 Munich
- **Phone:** +49 89 76756565
- **Website:** www.substanz-club.de
- **Opening Hours:** Events usually start around 8:00 PM; check the website for the current schedule.
- **Atmosphere:** Laid-back and alternative, with a focus on live performances and themed nights.

2. Bahnwärter Thiel

Overview:

Bahnwärter Thiel is one of Munich's most unique and creative venues, located in a former train yard in the Schlachthofviertel district. This open-air space is a hub for alternative culture, hosting everything from art exhibitions and flea markets to electronic music parties and outdoor cinema nights. The venue is constructed from shipping containers and old train cars, giving it an industrial, bohemian vibe.

What to Expect:

At Bahnwärter Thiel, you can expect a truly eclectic experience. The venue's program is constantly changing, offering a mix of cultural events, music performances, and community gatherings. Whether you're dancing to electronic beats, browsing through vintage clothing at a market, or watching an indie film under the stars, Bahnwärter Thiel provides a one-of-a-kind night out. The venue's creative atmosphere attracts a diverse crowd, making it a great place to meet like-minded people and discover something new.

Contact and Information:

- **Address:** Tumblingerstraße 29, 80337 Munich
- **Website:** www.bahnwaerterthiel.de
- **Atmosphere:** Creative and bohemian, with a focus on alternative culture and community events.

3. Glockenbachwerkstatt

Overview:

Glockenbachwerkstatt is a cultural center and alternative venue located in the heart of the Glockenbachviertel district. This community-oriented space hosts a wide range of events, including live music, film screenings, art exhibitions, and workshops. The venue has a relaxed, DIY atmosphere and is known for its inclusive and welcoming vibe.

What to Expect:

Glockenbachwerkstatt offers a diverse program that reflects the interests and creativity of the local community. You might find yourself attending a punk rock concert one night and a documentary film screening the next. The venue's bar serves affordable drinks, and the outdoor courtyard is a great place to hang out and chat with friends. Glockenbachwerkstatt is the perfect spot for those looking to explore Munich's alternative arts scene and connect with the local creative community.

Contact and Information:
- **Address:** Blumenstraße 7, 80331 Munich
- **Phone:** +49 89 2607395
- **Website:** www.glockenbachwerkstatt.de
- **Atmosphere:** DIY and community-focused, with a diverse range of cultural events.

Chapter 11: Seasonal Events and Festivals in Munich

A. Oktoberfest

Oktoberfest is synonymous with Munich and is, without a doubt, the city's most famous event. Known as the world's largest beer festival, Oktoberfest attracts millions of visitors from around the globe who come to experience the unparalleled combination of Bavarian tradition, culture, and, of course, beer. Held annually from late September to the first weekend in October, this iconic festival is a must-visit for anyone traveling to Munich during the autumn season. Here's everything you need to know to make the most of your Oktoberfest experience.

A Brief History of Oktoberfest

Oktoberfest dates back to October 12, 1810, when Crown Prince Ludwig of Bavaria (later King

Ludwig I) married Princess Therese of Saxony-Hildburghausen. The citizens of Munich were invited to join in the festivities, which included a grand horse race. The event was such a success that it became an annual tradition, eventually evolving into the Oktoberfest we know today. Over the years, the festival has expanded to include amusement rides, games, and, of course, massive beer tents.

Location: Theresienwiese

Oktoberfest takes place at Theresienwiese, a large open space near Munich's city center. The name Theresienwiese (meaning "Theresa's Meadow") honors Princess Therese, the bride in the royal wedding that started the festival. The area, often referred to simply as "Wiesn" by locals, is transformed into a bustling festival ground each year, with massive beer tents, food stalls, amusement rides, and more.

How to Get There:

- **By Public Transport:** The easiest way to reach Theresienwiese is by using Munich's excellent public transport system. The U4 and U5 U-Bahn lines stop directly at Theresienwiese station. Alternatively, the U3 and U6 lines stop at Goetheplatz or Poccistraße, both within walking distance of the festival grounds.

- **By Foot:** If you're staying in the city center, it's a pleasant walk to Theresienwiese from areas like Marienplatz or Karlsplatz.

The Beer Tents

The heart of Oktoberfest is the beer tents, each operated by one of Munich's famous breweries, including Augustiner, Paulaner, Hofbräu, and Löwenbräu, among others. These tents range in size, with the largest accommodating up to 10,000 people. Each tent has its own unique atmosphere, décor, and specialties, but they all share a common theme: serving up massive amounts of beer, traditional Bavarian food, and a whole lot of fun.

What to Expect:
- **Beer:** Oktoberfest beers are special brews made specifically for the festival, slightly stronger than your average beer with an alcohol content of around 6%. Beer is served in one-liter mugs known as "Maß." It's customary to toast with a hearty "Prost!" before taking your first sip.
- **Food:** The beer tents also serve a variety of traditional Bavarian dishes, including pretzels (Brezn), roast chicken (Hendl), pork knuckles (Schweinshaxe), sausages (Würstl), and more. Vegetarian options are also available, such as cheese plates (Käseplatte) and potato dumplings (Kartoffelknödel).

- **Music and Entertainment:** Each beer tent features live music, typically oompah bands playing traditional Bavarian tunes, along with popular songs that get the whole tent singing and dancing. The atmosphere is lively, with visitors often standing on benches, clinking glasses, and joining in on the fun.

Tips for Visiting the Beer Tents:
- **Arrive Early:** The beer tents fill up quickly, especially on weekends and public holidays. If you want a seat, it's best to arrive early in the day, particularly if you're in a large group.
- **Reservations:** Some tents allow table reservations, but these need to be made months in advance. If you have a reservation, be sure to arrive on time, as tables are often given away if the party doesn't show up promptly.
- **Bring Cash:** While some tents accept credit cards, it's easier and faster to pay in cash, especially for smaller purchases like drinks and snacks.

Beyond the Beer Tents

While the beer tents are the main attraction, there's much more to Oktoberfest. The festival grounds are home to a wide array of activities, including carnival rides, games, and shopping stalls.

Amusement Rides and Attractions:

Oktoberfest features a mix of traditional rides, such as the Ferris wheel and the classic "Krinoline" carousel, along with more modern attractions like roller coasters and haunted houses. These rides are great for taking a break from the beer tents and enjoying some family-friendly fun.

Traditional Costume:

Many visitors, both locals and tourists, choose to wear traditional Bavarian attire during Oktoberfest. Men typically wear Lederhosen (leather shorts with suspenders), while women wear Dirndls (traditional dresses with aprons). If you want to fully embrace the experience, consider renting or purchasing traditional clothing before heading to the festival.

Oide Wiesn:

For a more traditional Oktoberfest experience, visit the Oide Wiesn (Old Oktoberfest) section, located on the southern end of the festival grounds. Here, you'll find historical rides, old-fashioned beer tents, and a more relaxed atmosphere that harkens back to the early days of the festival. Entry to Oide Wiesn requires a small fee, but it's well worth it for the nostalgic ambiance.

Practical Information

Cost:

- **Entry:** Entry to Oktoberfest and the beer tents is free. However, you'll need to pay for food, drinks, and rides.

- **Beer Prices:** Expect to pay around €12-€13 for a Maß of beer. Prices for food vary depending on the dish and the tent.

Best Time to Visit:
The first weekend of Oktoberfest is typically the busiest, as it includes the grand parade and the official tapping of the first keg by the Mayor of Munich. For a less crowded experience, consider visiting during the weekdays, particularly in the mornings or early afternoons.

Safety Tips:
- **Stay Hydrated:** With all the beer drinking, it's important to stay hydrated. Be sure to drink water between beers and pace yourself to avoid overindulging.
- **Know Your Limits:** Oktoberfest can be overwhelming, especially if you're not used to drinking large quantities of beer. It's perfectly fine to take breaks, explore the festival grounds, or call it a night early if needed.

B. Christmas Markets

The Main Christmas Market at Marienplatz

Overview:
The heart of Munich's Christmas celebrations is the Christkindlmarkt at Marienplatz, the city's central square. This historic market dates back to the 14th century and is one of the oldest and most famous

Christmas markets in Germany. Set against the backdrop of the stunning New Town Hall (Neues Rathaus), this market exudes a timeless charm that captivates both locals and visitors alike.

What to Expect:

- **Stalls and Shopping:** The market features over 150 wooden stalls selling a wide variety of gifts, decorations, and handmade crafts. You'll find everything from intricately carved wooden ornaments and nativity scenes to woolen hats, scarves, and beautiful glassware. The market is also a great place to pick up traditional Bavarian gifts, such as gingerbread hearts (Lebkuchenherzen) and wooden toys.
- **Food and Drink:** No visit to the Christmas market is complete without indulging in some festive treats. Warm up with a mug of Glühwein (mulled wine), available in both red and white varieties, often spiced with cinnamon, cloves, and citrus. For something heartier, try a bratwurst, roasted chestnuts, or freshly baked pretzels. Don't miss out on the sweet options, like candied almonds (Gebrannte Mandeln) and stollen, a traditional German fruitcake dusted with powdered sugar.
- **The Christmas Tree:** The centerpiece of the Marienplatz market is the towering Christmas tree, adorned with thousands of lights and decorations. It creates a magical focal point for the market, making it an ideal

spot for photos or simply soaking in the festive atmosphere.

- **Live Music and Entertainment:** Throughout the Advent season, the market hosts live performances, including traditional Bavarian music, Christmas carols, and concerts from the balcony of the New Town Hall. These performances add to the joyful atmosphere and are a lovely way to experience the local culture.

Contact and Information:

- **Location:** Marienplatz, 80331 Munich
- **How to Get There:** Marienplatz is easily accessible by U-Bahn (U3, U6) and S-Bahn (all lines). The market is right in the city center, making it a convenient stop during your exploration of Munich.
- **Opening Hours:** The market typically runs from late November until Christmas Eve, with daily opening hours from 10:00 AM to 9:00 PM.
- **Website:** www.muenchen.de

The Medieval Christmas Market at Wittelsbacherplatz

Overview:

For a unique twist on the traditional Christmas market, visit the Medieval Christmas Market at Wittelsbacherplatz. This market transports you back to the Middle Ages, with vendors dressed in period costumes, medieval music playing in the background, and stalls selling handcrafted goods inspired by the era. The atmosphere is both festive and historical, offering a different kind of Christmas experience.

What to Expect:
- **Stalls and Shopping:** The market's stalls are designed to resemble medieval huts, where artisans sell handmade goods such as leather pouches, wooden toys, pottery, and jewelry. You can also watch blacksmiths and other craftsmen at work, demonstrating traditional techniques.
- **Food and Drink:** The culinary offerings at the Medieval Christmas Market are as unique as the market itself. Try a mug of hot mead (Met), a honey-based alcoholic drink that was popular in medieval times. You'll also find hearty dishes like roast pork sandwiches, grilled sausages, and hearty stews, all cooked over open fires.
- **Entertainment:** The market features live entertainment, including fire shows, sword-fighting demonstrations, and performances by minstrels and jugglers. These acts add to the immersive experience and are fun for both adults and children.

Contact and Information:
- **Location:** Wittelsbacherplatz, 80333 Munich

- **How to Get There:** The market is a short walk from the Odeonsplatz U-Bahn station (U4, U5).
- **Opening Hours:** The market usually operates from late November until just before Christmas, with daily hours from 11:00 AM to 9:00 PM.
- **Website:** www.mittelaltermarkt-muenchen.de

The Christmas Village at the Munich Residenz

Overview:

Nestled within the courtyard of the Munich Residenz, the Christmas Village (Weihnachtsdorf) offers a cozy and intimate setting for holiday shopping and festivities. Surrounded by the historic architecture of the former royal palace, this market feels like a small, enchanted village, complete with a nativity scene and plenty of charm.

What to Expect:

- **Stalls and Shopping:** The Christmas Village features a range of stalls offering high-quality gifts, including handmade candles, glass ornaments, and other artisanal products. The setting within the Residenz courtyard adds a touch of elegance and makes for a peaceful shopping experience away from the hustle and bustle of the larger markets.

- **Food and Drink:** Enjoy traditional Bavarian Christmas treats like sausages, roasted chestnuts, and Glühwein as you wander through the market. The atmosphere here is quieter and more relaxed, making it a great place to enjoy a leisurely meal or snack.
- **Children's Activities:** The Christmas Village is particularly family-friendly, with activities like a small carousel and a visit from St. Nicholas. The nativity scene, featuring live animals, is a highlight for children and adds to the festive spirit.

Contact and Information:
- **Location:** Residenzstraße 1, 80333 Munich
- **How to Get There:** The Munich Residenz is centrally located, just a short walk from the Odeonsplatz U-Bahn station (U4, U5).
- **Opening Hours:** The Christmas Village typically runs from late November to late December, with daily hours from 11:00 AM to 9:00 PM.
- **Website:** www.muenchner-weihnachtsdorf.de

The Tollwood Winter Festival

Overview:
For those looking for a more alternative and eclectic Christmas market experience, the Tollwood Winter Festival is a must-visit. Located at Theresienwiese,

the same site as Oktoberfest, Tollwood combines a Christmas market with a cultural festival, featuring a mix of international cuisine, art, live performances, and sustainable shopping options.

What to Expect:

- **Stalls and Shopping:** Tollwood is known for its focus on sustainability and fair trade, with stalls selling handmade crafts, organic products, and unique gifts from around the world. It's the perfect place to find eco-friendly and ethically sourced Christmas presents.
- **Food and Drink:** The festival offers a wide range of international foods, from vegan and vegetarian dishes to exotic street food. There's something for every taste, and the diverse options make it a great place to try something new.
- **Cultural Program:** Tollwood's cultural offerings include live music, theatre performances, art installations, and even a circus. The festival's tents host a variety of events, ranging from concerts by local bands to performances by international artists. The atmosphere is vibrant and multicultural, making it a unique addition to Munich's Christmas festivities.

Contact and Information:

- **Location:** Theresienwiese, 80336 Munich

- **How to Get There:** Theresienwiese is easily accessible by U-Bahn (U4, U5) with a stop directly at the festival grounds.
- **Opening Hours:** The Tollwood Winter Festival typically runs from late November to December 23rd, with daily hours from 2:00 PM to 11:00 PM.
- **Website:** www.tollwood.de

Practical Tips for Visiting Munich's Christmas Markets

Timing:
- **When to Visit:** The best time to visit Munich's Christmas markets is during the weekdays or earlier in the day to avoid the biggest crowds. Evenings, especially on weekends, can be very busy, but they also offer the most magical atmosphere with all the lights and decorations fully illuminated.
- **Weather Considerations:** Munich can be quite cold in December, so dress warmly with layers, gloves, and a hat. Comfortable shoes are also recommended, as you'll likely be doing a lot of walking.

What to Bring:
- **Cash:** While some stalls may accept credit cards, it's a good idea to carry cash for smaller purchases. Many of the traditional vendors prefer cash payments.

- **Reusable Mug:** Many Christmas markets charge a deposit for the mugs used for Glühwein and other hot drinks. You can either return the mug for a refund or keep it as a souvenir. Bringing a reusable mug can also be a more sustainable option.

Language:
- **German Phrases:** While many vendors speak English, knowing a few basic German phrases can enhance your experience. "Frohe Weihnachten" means "Merry Christmas," and "Ein Glühwein, bitte" will get you a delicious mulled wine.

C. Spring Festivals

Starkbierfest

Overview:
Starkbierfest, also known as the Strong Beer Festival, is one of Munich's best-kept secrets. Held during Lent, typically from mid-March to early April, this festival is a celebration of Starkbier, a type of strong beer originally brewed by monks to sustain themselves during the fasting period. Starkbierfest has a more intimate and traditional atmosphere than Oktoberfest, with many locals considering it the true Bavarian beer festival.

What to Expect:
- **Starkbier:** The star of the festival is, of course, Starkbier, which is a dark, malty

beer with a higher alcohol content than regular beers, often around 7-9%. Each of Munich's major breweries produces its own version of Starkbier, with some of the most famous being Paulaner's Salvator, Augustiner's Maximator, and Löwenbräu's Triumphator. The beers are typically served in 1-liter mugs (Maß), similar to those at Oktoberfest.

- **Traditional Food:** Alongside the strong beer, you'll find plenty of hearty Bavarian dishes to enjoy, such as roast pork (Schweinebraten), pretzels, sausages, and cheese plates (Brotzeit). The food is perfect for soaking up the strong beer and adds to the festive atmosphere.

- **Music and Entertainment:** Starkbierfest features live Bavarian music, with traditional oompah bands playing everything from folk tunes to popular drinking songs. The mood is lively, with plenty of singing, dancing, and toasting among the festival-goers. Some of the venues also host competitions and traditional performances, adding to the fun.

Top Venues:

- **Paulaner am Nockherberg:** The most famous location for Starkbierfest is Paulaner am Nockherberg, where the festival has been celebrated for centuries. This large beer hall and garden are filled with locals enjoying Paulaner's Salvator beer, and the atmosphere is friendly and welcoming.

- **Löwenbräukeller:** Another popular venue is the Löwenbräukeller, located near the Stiglmaierplatz. Here you can sample Löwenbräu's Triumphator while enjoying live music and a more traditional Bavarian setting.
- **Augustiner Keller:** For a more local experience, head to Augustiner Keller, where you can try their Maximator beer in a cozy beer hall or the expansive beer garden if the weather is mild.

Contact and Information:

- **Location:** Various locations throughout Munich, including Paulaner am Nockherberg, Löwenbräukeller, and Augustiner Keller.
- **How to Get There:** All major venues are easily accessible by public transport. Paulaner am Nockherberg is a short walk from the Kolumbusplatz U-Bahn station (U1, U2), Löwenbräukeller is near Stiglmaierplatz (U1), and Augustiner Keller is close to the Hauptbahnhof (main train station).
- **Opening Hours:** Starkbierfest usually runs from mid-March to early April. Check the specific venue websites for exact dates and times.

- **Website:**
  [www.muenchen.de](https://www.muenchen
  .de) (for general information)

Frühlingsfest

Overview:
Often referred to as the "little sister" of Oktoberfest,
Frühlingsfest (Spring Festival) is a popular event
that takes place in late April to early May at
Theresienwiese, the same grounds that host
Oktoberfest. Frühlingsfest is a family-friendly
festival with a more relaxed atmosphere, featuring
traditional beer tents, amusement rides, and a
variety of food stalls. It's a great way to enjoy the
festive spirit of Munich without the massive crowds
of Oktoberfest.

What to Expect:
- **Beer Tents:** Frühlingsfest features several
  beer tents, each offering a selection of
  Munich's best beers. The tents are smaller
  and less crowded than those at Oktoberfest,
  making it easier to find a seat and enjoy a
  Maß of beer. Popular tents include Festhalle
  Bayernland and Hippodrom, both of which
  offer live music and traditional Bavarian
  hospitality.
- **Rides and Attractions:** Frühlingsfest has a
  wide array of amusement rides, including a
  Ferris wheel, roller coasters, and classic
  fairground attractions like bumper cars and a
  haunted house. There's also a large flea

market held on the opening weekend, where you can browse for antiques, vintage items, and unique souvenirs.

- **Fireworks:** One of the highlights of Frühlingsfest is the fireworks display, which takes place on the two Friday evenings during the festival. The fireworks light up the night sky over Theresienwiese, creating a magical atmosphere for visitors.

Contact and Information:
- **Location:** Theresienwiese, 80336 Munich
- **How to Get There:** Theresienwiese is easily accessible by U-Bahn (U4, U5) with a station directly at the festival grounds.
- **Opening Hours:** Frühlingsfest typically runs from late April to early May. The beer tents are open from 10:00 AM to 11:00 PM (weekdays) and from 9:00 AM to 11:00 PM (weekends).
- **Website:** www.fruehlingsfest-muenchen.de

Auer Dult

Overview:
Auer Dult is a traditional Bavarian fair that takes place three times a year, with the spring edition known as the "Maidult" happening in early May. Held at Mariahilfplatz in the Au-Haidhausen district, Auer Dult is a charming blend of market,

fair, and folk festival, offering a more laid-back alternative to the larger beer festivals.

What to Expect:

- **Market Stalls:** Auer Dult is famous for its market, where vendors sell a wide variety of goods, including ceramics, kitchenware, antiques, and traditional crafts. It's the perfect place to find unique Bavarian souvenirs or simply browse the eclectic offerings.
- **Food and Drink:** The fair features numerous food stalls serving traditional Bavarian snacks and sweets, such as Steckerlfisch (grilled fish on a stick), sausages, pretzels, and Schmalznudeln (a type of fried dough). Beer and other beverages are available at several small beer gardens scattered throughout the fairground.
- **Rides and Entertainment:** Auer Dult also includes a few family-friendly amusement rides, such as a carousel and a small Ferris wheel. The atmosphere is relaxed, making it a great place to spend an afternoon with friends or family.

Contact and Information:

- **Location:** Mariahilfplatz, 81541 Munich
- **How to Get There:** The fairground is accessible by tram (Line 17 to Mariahilfplatz) or a short walk from the Rosenheimer Platz S-Bahn station.

- **Opening Hours:** Auer Dult runs from the last Saturday in April to the first Sunday in May. The market is open daily from 10:00 AM to 8:00 PM.
- **Website:** www.auerdult.de

Other Spring Events

- **Easter Markets:** In the weeks leading up to Easter, Munich hosts several Easter markets, where you can find beautifully decorated eggs, spring flowers, and Easter-themed crafts. The most popular Easter market is held at Marienplatz, featuring live music and special activities for children.
- **Maibaumfest:** On May 1st, many villages and neighborhoods in Munich celebrate the traditional Maibaumfest, where a maypole (Maibaum) is erected and decorated with ribbons and wreaths. The festivities often include traditional music, dancing, and plenty of food and drink, creating a lively and colorful celebration of spring.

Practical Tips for Visiting Munich's Spring Festivals

Weather:
Spring in Munich can be unpredictable, with temperatures ranging from chilly to mild. It's best to dress in layers and be prepared for rain, especially if you plan to visit one of the outdoor festivals.

What to Bring:
- **Comfortable Shoes:** You'll likely be doing a lot of walking, especially at festivals like Auer Dult or Frühlingsfest. Comfortable shoes are a must.
- **Cash:** While some vendors may accept credit cards, it's always a good idea to carry cash, especially for smaller purchases at market stalls or food stands.

Language:
German is the official language, but many vendors and staff at the festivals speak English. Learning a few basic German phrases, such as "Ein Bier, bitte" (A beer, please) or "Dankeschön" (Thank you), can enhance your experience.

D. Summer in Munich

1. Tollwood Summer Festival

Overview:
The Tollwood Summer Festival is one of Munich's most popular and eclectic events, held annually from late June to mid-July at the Olympiapark. This cultural festival is a celebration of diversity, sustainability, and creativity, offering a unique blend of music, art, food, and performances. The festival's focus on environmental consciousness makes it a favorite among those who appreciate green living and cultural exchange.

What to Expect:

- **Live Music and Performances:** Tollwood features an impressive lineup of concerts and performances, with genres ranging from rock and pop to world music and jazz. The festival attracts both local and international artists, with live music taking place on multiple stages throughout the festival grounds. In addition to concerts, you'll find dance performances, theatre shows, and circus acts that cater to all ages.

- **Market of Ideas:** The festival's Market of Ideas is a sprawling marketplace where you can browse stalls selling handmade crafts, eco-friendly products, and international goods. The market is a great place to find unique souvenirs, clothing, jewelry, and art, all while supporting local artisans and sustainable businesses.

- **Food and Drink:** Tollwood offers a diverse range of food options, with an emphasis on organic and fair-trade ingredients. You can sample cuisine from around the world, including vegetarian and vegan dishes, as well as traditional Bavarian specialties. There's also a wide selection of drinks, including organic beer, wine, and cocktails.

- **Environmental Awareness:** One of the key themes of Tollwood is environmental awareness. The festival promotes sustainability through various initiatives, including waste reduction, renewable energy use, and educational workshops on topics like climate change and green living.

Contact and Information:

- **Location:** Olympiapark, Spiridon-Louis-Ring 21, 80809 Munich
- **How to Get There:** The festival is easily accessible by U-Bahn (U3 to Olympiazentrum) or by tram (Lines 20 and 21).
- **Opening Hours:** Tollwood typically runs from late June to mid-July, with the market and food stalls open daily from 2:00 PM to midnight. Concert times vary, so check the schedule on the website.
- **Website:** www.tollwood.de

2. Kocherlball

Overview:

The Kocherlball is one of Munich's most charming and unique traditions, taking place early in the morning on a Sunday in July at the Chinese Tower (Chinesischer Turm) in the Englischer Garten. The event dates back to the 19th century when Munich's servants, cooks, and other workers would gather before dawn to dance and socialize before starting their day. The tradition was revived in 1989 and has since become a beloved summer event.

What to Expect:

- **Traditional Bavarian Dance:** The highlight of the Kocherlball is the traditional Bavarian dancing, with participants dressed in Dirndls and Lederhosen performing folk dances like the Schuhplattler and Polka. A live band plays traditional Bavarian music, creating a festive and nostalgic atmosphere.
- **Early Start:** The event begins very early, with people arriving as early as 5:00 AM to secure a good spot. Dancing usually starts around 6:00 AM and continues until about 10:00 AM. Despite the early hour, the Kocherlball draws a large crowd, with both locals and tourists eager to take part in the fun.
- **Picnic Breakfast:** Many attendees bring a picnic breakfast to enjoy during the event. It's common to see tables set with traditional Bavarian foods like pretzels, sausages, and cheese, along with coffee or a morning beer. The communal spirit of the event is one of its most appealing aspects, as people share food, stories, and laughter in the early morning light.

Contact and Information:
- **Location:** Chinesischer Turm, Englischer Garten, 80538 Munich
- **How to Get There:** The Chinese Tower is located in the Englischer Garten, accessible by tram (Line 18 to Tivolistraße) or by foot from the Universität or Giselastraße U-Bahn stations.

- **Opening Hours:** The Kocherlball usually takes place on a Sunday in July, with festivities starting around 6:00 AM and ending by 10:00 AM. Check local listings for the exact date each year.
- **Website:** www.muenchen.de

3. Munich Summer Olympics (Sommer in der Stadt)

Overview:
Sommer in der Stadt, or "Summer in the City," is a relatively new initiative launched by the city of Munich to provide locals and visitors with a wide range of outdoor activities and entertainment throughout the summer months. Spread across various locations in the city, this event includes everything from open-air concerts and sports activities to pop-up beer gardens and cultural performances. It's a great way to enjoy the summer atmosphere in Munich, with something for everyone to enjoy.

What to Expect:
- **Open-Air Concerts:** Throughout the summer, various open-air concerts are held in public spaces like Königsplatz, Olympiapark, and Marienplatz. These concerts feature a diverse lineup of music, including classical, jazz, pop, and rock, often with free entry.

- **Sports and Activities:** Sommer in der Stadt offers numerous sports activities, including beach volleyball, skateboarding, and climbing walls. These activities are set up in parks and public squares, providing opportunities for people of all ages to participate.
- **Pop-Up Beer Gardens:** No summer event in Munich would be complete without beer gardens. During Sommer in der Stadt, several pop-up beer gardens appear throughout the city, offering a relaxed place to enjoy a cold beer, traditional Bavarian food, and the warm summer evenings.
- **Cultural Performances:** The event also includes a variety of cultural performances, such as theatre, dance, and art installations. These performances take place in parks and public spaces, making culture accessible to everyone in a relaxed, open-air setting.

Contact and Information:
- **Location:** Various locations throughout Munich, including Olympiapark, Königsplatz, and Marienplatz.
- **How to Get There:** The event takes place across multiple locations, all easily accessible by public transport.
- **Opening Hours:** Sommer in der Stadt typically runs from late June to early September, with different activities and performances scheduled throughout the summer.

- **Website:**
  [www.muenchen.de](https://www.muenchen
  .de)

4. Kaltenberg Medieval Tournament

Overview:
Located just outside of Munich in the town of
Kaltenberg, the Kaltenberg Medieval Tournament is
a spectacular summer event that transports visitors
back to the Middle Ages. Held over several
weekends in July, this festival features jousting
tournaments, medieval markets, and live
entertainment, all set against the backdrop of the
historic Kaltenberg Castle.

What to Expect:
- **Jousting Tournament:** The centerpiece of
  the Kaltenberg Medieval Tournament is the
  thrilling jousting competition, where knights
  in full armor compete in a display of skill
  and bravery. The tournament is a dramatic
  spectacle, complete with charging horses,
  clashing swords, and cheering crowds.
- **Medieval Market:** The festival also
  features a large medieval market, where
  vendors sell handcrafted goods, medieval
  clothing, and traditional foods. You can
  browse through stalls offering everything
  from swords and armor to leather goods and
  jewelry, all while enjoying the sights and
  sounds of medieval life.

- **Entertainment and Performances:** In addition to the jousting, the festival offers a wide range of live entertainment, including minstrels, jugglers, fire-eaters, and acrobats. There are also reenactments of historical events, storytelling, and workshops where you can learn about medieval crafts and skills.

Contact and Information:
- **Location:** Kaltenberg Castle, 82269 Geltendorf (approximately 45 minutes from Munich)
- **How to Get There:** Kaltenberg is accessible by car or by taking a regional train from Munich to Geltendorf, followed by a short bus ride to the castle.
- **Opening Hours:** The tournament takes place on weekends in July. Gates typically open at 11:00 AM, with events running throughout the day.
- **Website:** www.ritterturnier.de

5. Open-Air Cinemas

Overview:
During the summer, Munich's open-air cinemas are a popular way to enjoy warm evenings under the stars. These cinemas screen a variety of films, from Hollywood blockbusters to classic movies and indie films, all in picturesque outdoor settings. It's a

relaxed and enjoyable way to spend a summer night in Munich, with friends, family, or even solo.

What to Expect:
- **Locations:** Some of the most popular open-air cinemas in Munich include Kino, Mond & Sterne at the Westpark lake, the open-air cinema at the Olympiapark, and the Filmfest München screenings in various locations across the city.
- **Film Selection:** The film selection varies by venue, but typically includes a mix of recent releases, classics, and international films. Screenings are usually in the original language with German subtitles, making it accessible to both locals and visitors.

E. Autumn Traditions and Harvest Celebrations

1. Kirchweihdult: The Autumn Auer Dult

Overview:
The Kirchweihdult, also known as the Autumn Auer Dult, is the last of the three annual Auer Dult fairs held at Mariahilfplatz in the Au-Haidhausen district. Taking place in October, this traditional Bavarian fair is a wonderful blend of market, folk festival, and family-friendly fun. The Kirchweihdult has a special charm in the autumn, with the crisp air and golden leaves adding to the festive atmosphere.

What to Expect:

- **Market Stalls:** Like the other Auer Dult fairs, the Kirchweihdult features a wide array of market stalls selling everything from ceramics and household goods to antiques and traditional crafts. It's an ideal place to find unique gifts, seasonal decorations, and handmade items that reflect Bavarian culture.
- **Traditional Food and Drink:** The food stalls at Kirchweihdult offer a variety of Bavarian specialties, including roasted almonds, sausages, pretzels, and seasonal dishes like roast goose. Warm up with a hot drink, such as mulled wine or freshly brewed coffee, as you browse the stalls or enjoy the rides.
- **Rides and Attractions:** The fair also includes several amusement rides, such as a Ferris wheel, carousel, and bumper cars, making it a fun outing for families. The atmosphere is festive yet relaxed, with plenty of opportunities to enjoy the sights and sounds of autumn in Munich.

Contact and Information:
- **Location:** Mariahilfplatz, 81541 Munich
- **How to Get There:** The fairground is accessible by tram (Line 17 to Mariahilfplatz) or a short walk from the Rosenheimer Platz S-Bahn station.
- **Opening Hours:** The Kirchweihdult typically takes place over nine days in

mid-October, with market hours from 10:00 AM to 8:00 PM.
- **Website:**
  www.auerdult.de

2. Erntedankfest: The Harvest Festival

Overview:
Erntedankfest, or the Harvest Festival, is a traditional German celebration that gives thanks for the year's bountiful harvest. While the exact date of the festival can vary, it is typically celebrated on the first Sunday in October. In Munich, Erntedankfest is observed with church services, parades, and special events that highlight the region's agricultural heritage and the importance of community.

What to Expect:
- **Church Services:** Many of Munich's churches hold special Erntedankfest services, where congregations give thanks for the harvest and pray for continued blessings. The churches are often decorated with harvest symbols, such as wheat sheaves, fruits, vegetables, and flowers, creating a beautiful and meaningful atmosphere.
- **Parades and Celebrations:** In some areas, Erntedankfest is marked by parades featuring floats decorated with harvest produce, traditional costumes, and folk music. These parades are a colorful and festive way to celebrate the season, bringing

together communities to honor their agricultural roots.

- **Harvest Markets:** Some districts in Munich hold harvest markets or fairs as part of the Erntedankfest celebrations. These markets offer fresh produce, artisanal goods, and seasonal foods, allowing visitors to experience the flavors and traditions of Bavarian autumn. It's a great opportunity to sample local specialties and purchase fresh, locally grown products.

Contact and Information:

- **Location:** Various locations throughout Munich, including churches and public squares.
- **How to Get There:** Check with local churches or community centers for specific event locations and times.
- **Opening Hours:** Erntedankfest is typically celebrated on the first Sunday in October, with events occurring throughout the day.
- **Website:** www.muenchen.de

3. Almabtrieb: The Cattle Drive

Overview:

Almabtrieb, also known as the Cattle Drive, is a traditional event that takes place in rural Bavaria during the autumn months, particularly in September and October. This event marks the return of cattle from the alpine pastures, where they have spent the summer grazing, to their farms in the valleys for the winter. While Almabtrieb is more commonly associated with the Bavarian Alps, you can also experience this tradition in areas surrounding Munich.

What to Expect:
- **Decorated Cattle:** The highlight of Almabtrieb is the sight of cattle adorned with colorful headdresses, flowers, and large bells as they are led through the streets by their herders. This procession is both a celebration of the successful summer grazing season and a way to bless the cattle before they are sheltered for the winter.
- **Festive Atmosphere:** Almabtrieb is often accompanied by local festivals, with music, dancing, and plenty of food and drink. These events bring together the community to celebrate the end of the agricultural season and the start of autumn. You'll find traditional Bavarian foods like sausages, cheese, and fresh bread, as well as locally brewed beer.
- **Regional Variations:** While Almabtrieb is celebrated throughout Bavaria, each region has its own unique customs and traditions. In some places, the event is a small, local affair, while in others, it's a large festival that attracts visitors from near and far. If you're interested in experiencing

Almabtrieb, it's worth checking the schedules of nearby towns and villages.

Contact and Information:
- **Location:** Various locations in Bavaria, with events occurring in rural areas around Munich.
- **How to Get There:** Depending on the location, you may need to drive or take a regional train to reach the Almabtrieb events.
- **Website:** www.bavaria.by (for general information about Almabtrieb in Bavaria)

4. Oktoberfest Closing Events

Overview:
While Oktoberfest officially takes place from late September to the first weekend in October, the final weekend of the festival is particularly special, featuring a series of closing events that are not to be missed. These events mark the end of the world's largest beer festival with a mix of tradition, celebration, and a touch of nostalgia.

What to Expect:
- **Gun Salute:** On the final day of Oktoberfest, a traditional gun salute (Böllerschießen) is held at noon on the steps of the Bavaria statue at Theresienwiese. This event features members of local shooting

clubs dressed in traditional attire, firing blank shots into the air to signal the close of the festival. It's a dramatic and symbolic way to bring the festivities to an end.

- **Final Beer Tents Toasts:** As the festival draws to a close, the atmosphere in the beer tents becomes especially lively, with final toasts, singing, and dancing. The last evening is a time for both celebration and reflection, as visitors raise their glasses one last time to the spirit of Oktoberfest. Many tents offer special closing ceremonies or performances, making it a memorable experience.
- **Bavarian Music and Farewell:** The closing night of Oktoberfest is filled with traditional Bavarian music, as bands play beloved folk songs and drinking anthems. The mood is festive, yet there's a sense of farewell as the festival comes to a close for another year. Visitors often join hands, swaying to the music, and singing along as they bid goodbye to Oktoberfest.

Contact and Information:
- **Location:** Theresienwiese, 80336 Munich
- **How to Get There:** Theresienwiese is easily accessible by U-Bahn (U4, U5) with a station directly at the festival grounds.
- **Opening Hours:** Oktoberfest's final weekend typically takes place in early October, with the closing events occurring on the last Sunday.

- **Website:**
  [www.oktoberfest.de](https://www.oktoberf
  est.de)

5. Wine Harvest Festivals (Weinfeste)

Overview:
In addition to beer, Bavaria is also known for its wine, particularly in the Franconian region to the north of Munich. During the autumn months, wine harvest festivals, or Weinfeste, are held to celebrate the grape harvest. These festivals offer a chance to taste local wines, enjoy traditional Bavarian food, and participate in various cultural activities.

What to Expect:
- **Wine Tasting:** The main attraction at any Weinfest is the wine, with local vineyards offering tastings of their best vintages. Franconian wine, known for its dry white varieties like Silvaner and Müller-Thurgau, is particularly popular. You'll have the opportunity to sample a wide range of wines, often paired with regional specialties like cheese, sausages, and bread.
- **Cultural Events:** Many wine harvest festivals include cultural events such as traditional music, folk dances, and parades. These events showcase the local heritage and provide a festive backdrop to the wine tasting. In some towns, the festivals are held in historic settings, such as castles or market squares, adding to the charm.

- **Autumn Scenery:** The wine regions of Bavaria are especially beautiful in the autumn, with vineyards turning shades of gold and red against the rolling hills. Many Weinfeste take place in these picturesque settings, allowing you to enjoy the stunning autumn scenery while savoring the local wines. Some festivals also offer guided vineyard tours, where you can learn more about the winemaking process and the history of the region.

Top Locations for Weinfeste:
- **Franconian Wine Region:** The Franconian region, located north of Munich, is home to some of Bavaria's best-known wine towns, such as Würzburg, Volkach, and Iphofen. These towns host some of the most popular Weinfeste in Bavaria, each with its own unique charm and traditions.
- **Munich and Surrounding Areas:** While Munich is more famous for its beer, the city and surrounding areas also host smaller Weinfeste during the autumn months. These festivals offer a more intimate experience and are a great way to explore Bavarian wine culture without traveling far from the city.

Contact and Information:
- **Location:** Various locations throughout Bavaria, particularly in the Franconian wine region.

- **How to Get There:** Depending on the festival location, you can travel by car or regional train. Franconian wine towns like Würzburg and Volkach are easily accessible from Munich.
- **Opening Hours:** Weinfeste typically take place in September and October, with dates varying by location. Check local tourism websites for specific festival dates and details.
- **Website:** www.franken-weinland.de (for information on Franconian wine festivals)

Practical Tips for Enjoying Autumn Festivals in Munich

Weather:
Autumn weather in Munich can be quite variable, with temperatures ranging from cool and crisp to chilly and damp. It's important to dress in layers and bring a jacket or coat, especially for outdoor events. Comfortable, weather-appropriate footwear is also recommended, as you'll likely be walking or standing for long periods.

What to Bring:
- **Cash:** While many larger festivals accept credit cards, it's always a good idea to carry cash, especially for smaller purchases at market stalls or food vendors.

- **Reusable Bags:** If you're planning to shop at any of the autumn markets or festivals, bringing a reusable bag is a practical way to carry your purchases and reduce waste.

Transportation:

Public transportation is the best way to get around Munich and to reach most festival locations. The city's U-Bahn, S-Bahn, trams, and buses are reliable and convenient. For festivals outside of Munich, such as those in the Franconian wine region, regional trains are a good option. If you're planning to attend events in rural areas, consider renting a car or checking for shuttle services provided by the festival.

Timing:

Autumn festivals in Munich can get crowded, especially on weekends. To make the most of your experience, consider visiting during the week or arriving early in the day. For events like the Almabtrieb or wine festivals, it's also a good idea to check the schedule in advance to catch the main attractions.

Chapter 12: Travel Tips and Practical Information

A. Language and Communication

Official Language: German

German is the official language of Munich and is used in all public and official settings, including signage, public transport, and at most businesses. The Bavarian dialect, known as "Bayerisch," is commonly spoken among locals, but standard German (Hochdeutsch) is widely understood and used, especially in professional and educational contexts.

Key German Phrases:
Learning a few basic German phrases can go a long way in helping you interact with locals and navigate the city. Here are some essential phrases to get you started:

Greetings and Basic Phrases

1. Guten Morgen
- Meaning: Good morning
- Pronunciation: GOO-ten MOR-gen

2. Servus
- Meaning: Hello (informal, common in Bavaria)
- Pronunciation: SAIR-voos

3. Danke schön
- Meaning: Thank you very much
- Pronunciation: DAHN-keh shurn

4. Entschuldigung
- Meaning: Excuse me / I'm sorry
- Pronunciation: Ent-SHOOL-dee-goong

Transportation

5. Wo ist der Bahnhof?
- Meaning: Where is the train station?
- Pronunciation: Voh ist dair BAHN-hof?

6. Wie viel kostet ein Ticket nach...?
- Meaning: How much is a ticket to...?
- Pronunciation: Vee feel KOH-stet ayn TIK-et nahkh...?

7. Ich möchte ein Taxi bestellen.
- Meaning: I would like to order a taxi.
- Pronunciation: Ikh MERKH-te ayn TAX-ee beh-SHTELL-en.

Dining and Ordering Food

8. Ich hätte gern ein Bier, bitte.
- Meaning: I would like a beer, please.
- Pronunciation: Ikh HET-te gairn ayn beer, BIT-te.

9. Die Speisekarte, bitte.

- Meaning: The menu, please.
- Pronunciation: Dee SHPY-zeh-kar-teh, BIT-te.

10. Was empfehlen Sie?

- Meaning: What do you recommend?
- Pronunciation: Vahs em-FAY-len zee?

Shopping

11. Wie viel kostet das?

- Meaning: How much does that cost?
- Pronunciation: Vee feel KOH-stet dahs?

12. Kann ich mit Karte zahlen?

- Meaning: Can I pay with a card?
- Pronunciation: Kahn ikh mit KAR-teh TSAH-len?

13. Haben Sie das in einer anderen Größe?

- Meaning: Do you have that in another size?
- Pronunciation: HAH-ben zee dahs in AY-ner AHN-dern GROY-seh?

Emergencies and Help

14. Hilfe!

- Meaning: Help!
- Pronunciation: HILL-feh!

15. Wo ist die nächste Apotheke?

- Meaning: Where is the nearest pharmacy?

- Pronunciation: Voh ist dee NAYKH-steh ah-poh-TAY-keh?

English Proficiency in Munich

While German is the primary language, English is widely spoken, particularly in areas frequented by tourists, such as hotels, restaurants, and major attractions. Many Munich residents, especially younger people and those working in the service industry, have a good command of English, so you should have little trouble communicating in most situations.

Where You'll Find English Speakers:
- **Hotels and Restaurants:** Staff in most hotels and restaurants in Munich are accustomed to dealing with international visitors and can usually communicate in English. Menus in tourist-heavy areas often include English translations.
- **Museums and Tourist Attractions:** Information at major tourist attractions and museums is often available in both German and English. Audio guides and guided tours are commonly offered in English as well.
- **Public Transport:** Announcements on Munich's U-Bahn and S-Bahn systems are typically made in German, but signage is often accompanied by English translations. Ticket machines also offer an English language option.

Communication Tips

While you can generally get by with English in Munich, showing an effort to speak a few words of German is always appreciated by locals. Here are some tips to help you communicate effectively:

- **Politeness Counts:** German culture values politeness and formality, especially when addressing strangers. It's customary to use "Sie" (the formal "you") when speaking with someone you don't know well, especially in professional or service contexts. Switching to the informal "du" is common among friends or in casual settings, but it's best to wait until invited to do so.
- **Body Language:** Germans typically value personal space and may not be as physically demonstrative as people from other cultures. Handshakes are the standard greeting, and a firm handshake with eye contact is considered polite. Avoid excessive hand gestures or touching during conversations.
- **Listen Carefully:** The Bavarian dialect can be challenging to understand, even for those who speak standard German. If you find it difficult to follow a conversation, don't hesitate to ask the person to repeat themselves or speak a bit more slowly. Most people will be happy to accommodate you.
- **Use Technology:** If you're unsure about your German language skills, consider using

a translation app on your smartphone. Apps like Google Translate can be invaluable for translating signs, menus, or short conversations on the go.

Signage and Information

Munich's public signage is primarily in German, but key areas such as train stations, airports, and tourist attractions often include English translations. Here's what you need to know about common signs and information:

- **Bahnhof:** Train station
- **Ausgang:** Exit
- **Eingang:** Entrance
- **Toilette:** Restroom
- **Notausgang:** Emergency exit
- **Information:** Information desk or tourist information
- **Polizei:** Police
- **Krankenhaus:** Hospital
- **Apotheke:** Pharmacy
- **Geschlossen:** Closed
- **Geöffnet:** Open

Language Assistance

If you find yourself in a situation where communication is challenging, don't hesitate to ask for help. Many people in Munich are willing to assist tourists, whether by providing directions, helping with translations, or offering recommendations.

Where to Seek Help:
- **Tourist Information Centers:** Located at key points around the city, such as Marienplatz and the Hauptbahnhof (main train station), these centers offer assistance in multiple languages and can provide maps, brochures, and advice.
- **Public Transport Staff:** U-Bahn and S-Bahn staff, particularly those at major stations, are accustomed to helping tourists and can assist with ticket purchases or directions.
- **Hotel Reception:** Hotel staff are often a great resource for language assistance, recommendations, and advice on navigating the city.

B. Currency and Money Matters

The Euro (€): Germany's Official Currency

The euro (€) is the official currency of Germany and 18 other European Union countries. Each euro is divided into 100 cents. The euro is available in both coins and banknotes:

- **Coins:** Coins are available in denominations of 1, 2, 5, 10, 20, and 50 cents, as well as €1 and €2.

- **Banknotes:** Banknotes come in denominations of €5, €10, €20, €50, €100, €200, and €500. However, larger notes like €200 and €500 are less commonly used in daily transactions.

Currency Symbols and Codes:
- **Symbol:** €
- **ISO Code:** EUR

Exchanging Currency

If you're arriving in Munich with a different currency, you'll need to exchange some of your money into euros. Here are some tips for currency exchange:

- **Airport Exchange Services:** Munich Airport (Franz Josef Strauss International Airport) has several currency exchange counters in both terminals. While convenient, these services often charge higher fees and offer less favorable exchange rates than other options.
- **Banks and Currency Exchange Offices:** Banks in Munich, such as Deutsche Bank, Commerzbank, and Sparkasse, offer currency exchange services. Currency exchange offices can also be found in the city center, especially near major tourist areas like Marienplatz and the Hauptbahnhof (main train station). These options typically offer better rates than

airport services but may charge a service fee.

- **ATMs:** One of the easiest and most cost-effective ways to get euros is by withdrawing cash from an ATM (Geldautomat). ATMs are widely available throughout Munich, including at the airport, train stations, and city streets. When using an ATM, it's important to check with your home bank about any foreign transaction fees that may apply. It's also advisable to use ATMs affiliated with major banks to avoid additional surcharges.

Tips for Currency Exchange:
- **Compare Rates:** Exchange rates can vary, so it's a good idea to compare rates at different exchange offices or banks before converting large amounts of money.
- **Avoid Airport Exchanges:** If possible, avoid exchanging large sums of money at the airport, as the rates are usually less favorable.
- **Use ATMs for Small Withdrawals:** If you only need a small amount of cash, withdrawing from an ATM can be a convenient option. Just be aware of any fees your bank may charge.

Credit and Debit Cards

Credit and debit cards are widely accepted in Munich, especially in hotels, restaurants, and larger stores. However, it's important to be aware that some smaller businesses, cafes, and markets may only accept cash, or have a minimum spending requirement for card payments.

Accepted Cards:
- **Visa and Mastercard:** These are the most commonly accepted credit cards in Munich. You can use them in most hotels, restaurants, shops, and ATMs.
- **American Express:** While accepted in many places, American Express may not be as widely accepted as Visa or Mastercard, particularly in smaller establishments.
- **Maestro and Cirrus:** Debit cards with the Maestro or Cirrus logo are also widely accepted at ATMs and some point-of-sale locations.

Using Cards in Munich:
- **PIN Required:** For most transactions, especially at ATMs, you'll need to enter your card's PIN (Personal Identification Number). Make sure you know your PIN before you travel.
- **Notify Your Bank:** Before traveling to Munich, inform your bank of your travel dates to avoid having your card blocked due to suspicious activity.
- **Check for Fees:** Some banks and credit card companies charge foreign transaction fees, usually around 1-3% of the transaction

amount. It's worth checking with your bank to understand any fees that may apply.

Cash vs. Card: When to Use Each

While Munich is increasingly moving toward a cashless society, cash is still king in many everyday transactions, particularly in smaller establishments and markets. Here's when to use cash and when to use a card:

Use Cash For:
- Small purchases at local markets, street vendors, or kiosks
- Tipping in restaurants, cafes, and taxis (though tipping can also be added to a card payment)
- Public transportation tickets, especially when buying from vending machines
- Entry fees at smaller museums or attractions that may not accept cards

Use Cards For:
- Hotel bookings and larger purchases at department stores
- Dining at mid-range to high-end restaurants
- Renting a car or making large travel-related payments
- Shopping at major retail chains or supermarkets

Carrying Cash:

It's a good idea to carry some cash with you at all times, especially for smaller purchases or when visiting areas where card payments may not be as readily accepted. As a general rule, €50-€100 in small denominations (such as €10 and €20 notes) is sufficient for most daily expenses.

Tipping and Service Charges

Tipping in Munich is appreciated but not mandatory, and it differs somewhat from tipping practices in the United States or other countries.

- **Restaurants:** In restaurants, it's customary to round up the bill or leave a small tip of about 5-10% for good service. For example, if your bill is €18.50, you might round up to €20. When paying by card, you can ask to add the tip to the total amount or leave it in cash. To tip, tell the server the total amount you'd like to pay, including the tip, when handing over the money.
- **Cafes and Bars:** In cafes and bars, rounding up the bill is common, or leaving a small tip of around €0.50 to €2 depending on the size of the order.
- **Taxis:** For taxi rides, rounding up to the nearest euro or adding a tip of around 5% is customary.
- **Hotels:** Tipping hotel staff, such as porters or housekeeping, is not required but appreciated. A tip of €1-€2 per bag for

porters or €1-€2 per day for housekeeping is a nice gesture.

Money-Saving Tips

Traveling in Munich doesn't have to break the bank. Here are some tips to help you manage your money and make the most of your budget:

- **Use Public Transport:** Munich's public transport system is efficient and affordable. Consider purchasing a day pass or a multi-day pass to save money on transportation.
- **Eat Like a Local:** Enjoying a meal at a local beer garden or a traditional Bavarian tavern (Wirtshaus) can be both affordable and delicious. Look for lunch specials (Mittagsmenü) offered by many restaurants during weekdays.
- **Free Attractions:** Many of Munich's parks, gardens, and churches are free to visit. English Garden, Marienplatz, and the Isar River are great places to explore without spending a dime.
- **Shop Smart:** If you're looking to buy souvenirs or gifts, consider shopping at local markets or smaller shops outside of the main tourist areas, where prices are often more reasonable.

C. Health and Safety

Healthcare in Munich

Munich has an excellent healthcare system, with numerous hospitals, clinics, and pharmacies (Apotheken) throughout the city. The standard of care is high, and medical professionals are well-trained, with many doctors and healthcare workers speaking English.

Emergency Services:
- **Emergency Number:** In case of a medical emergency, dial 112 for an ambulance. This number is toll-free and can be dialed from any phone, including mobiles. It connects you to emergency services, including medical, fire, and police.
- **Hospital Emergency Rooms (Notaufnahme):** If you need immediate medical attention but it's not life-threatening, you can go directly to the emergency room (Notaufnahme) at any major hospital. Two of the main hospitals in Munich with emergency services include:
- **Klinikum der Universität München (LMU) – Großhadern Campus:** Marchioninistraße 15, 81377 Munich. Phone: +49 89 440050.
- **Klinikum rechts der Isar – Technische Universität München:** Ismaninger Str. 22, 81675 Munich. Phone: +49 89 41400.

Pharmacies (Apotheken):

Pharmacies in Munich are widely available and easy to spot by their red "A" sign. Most pharmacies are open Monday to Saturday from around 8:00 AM to 6:00 PM. Some pharmacies offer extended hours or are open 24/7, especially those located near major train stations.

If you need medication outside of regular hours, look for the "Notdienst" sign at any pharmacy, which lists the nearest open pharmacy during nights and weekends.

Health Insurance:
- **Travel Insurance:** It's highly recommended that you purchase travel health insurance before your trip to cover any unexpected medical expenses. If you're a citizen of the European Union (EU), European Economic Area (EEA), or Switzerland, your European Health Insurance Card (EHIC) will allow you to access public healthcare at the same cost as local residents.
- **Private Insurance:** If you have private health insurance, check with your provider about coverage in Germany. Most private insurance plans cover emergency medical care, but it's important to understand the specifics of your policy.

Safety in Munich

Munich is considered one of the safest cities in Germany, with low crime rates and a strong police presence. However, like any major city, it's important to stay vigilant and take basic precautions to ensure your safety.

General Safety Tips:
- **Pickpocketing:** Pickpocketing can occur in crowded areas, such as public transport, tourist attractions, and markets. Keep your valuables secure and be aware of your surroundings, especially in busy places. Consider using a money belt or keeping your wallet in a front pocket.
- **Public Transport:** Munich's public transport system is safe and reliable, even late at night. However, it's always a good idea to stay in well-lit areas and be mindful of your belongings.
- **Solo Travel:** Munich is a safe city for solo travelers, including women. It's generally safe to walk around at night, especially in central areas. However, exercise the same caution you would in any unfamiliar city, such as avoiding poorly lit or deserted areas.
- **Emergency Number:** For police assistance, dial 110. This number is toll-free and connects you directly to the local police.

Natural Hazards:
- **Weather:** Munich experiences a temperate climate, but weather can be unpredictable, especially in the winter months. Be prepared for rain, snow, or sudden temperature drops

by dressing in layers and carrying an umbrella.

- **Flooding:** While rare, heavy rains can cause localized flooding, particularly near the Isar River. If you're visiting during the rainy season, stay informed about weather conditions and avoid areas prone to flooding.

Local Laws and Customs:

- **Drinking Age:** The legal drinking age in Munich is 16 for beer and wine and 18 for spirits. Public drinking is generally accepted, especially in beer gardens and during festivals. However, it's important to drink responsibly and be mindful of local customs.
- **Smoking:** Smoking is prohibited in indoor public spaces, including restaurants, bars, and public transport. Designated smoking areas are available outside most establishments.
- **Public Behavior:** Munich values orderliness and respect for public spaces. Littering, jaywalking, and loud behavior, especially late at night, are frowned upon. It's also important to respect local customs, such as standing on the right side of escalators to allow others to pass.

D. Local Etiquette and Customs

Greetings and Social Etiquette

Greetings:

In Munich, greetings are an important part of social interactions. A polite greeting can set a positive tone for any encounter, whether you're meeting someone for the first time or interacting with service staff.

- **Handshakes:** A firm handshake is the standard greeting in Munich when meeting someone for the first time or in formal situations. It's customary to make eye contact and smile while shaking hands.
- **"Grüß Gott":** In Bavaria, it's common to greet people with "Grüß Gott" (literally "God greet you"), especially in more traditional or rural areas. This phrase is a friendly and respectful way to say hello. You can also use the standard German "Guten Tag" (Good day) or "Hallo" (Hello) for a more casual greeting.
- **Addressing People:** In formal settings, it's polite to use titles and last names (e.g., Herr Müller or Frau Schmidt) until invited to use first names. In less formal situations, first names are often used more quickly, especially among younger people.

Respect for Personal Space:

Germans, including Bavarians, typically value personal space and may maintain a bit more distance in social interactions compared to other cultures. It's important to respect this by not standing too close or touching others unnecessarily.

Punctuality:
Punctuality is highly valued in Munich. Whether you're meeting friends, attending a business meeting, or arriving for a reservation, being on time is seen as a sign of respect and reliability. If you're running late, it's courteous to inform the person or establishment as soon as possible.

Dining Etiquette

Dining in Munich offers a wonderful opportunity to experience Bavarian hospitality and cuisine. Understanding local dining customs can make your meal more enjoyable and help you navigate social situations with ease.

Table Manners:
- **Seating:** In many traditional Bavarian beer gardens, it's common to share tables with strangers, especially during busy times. It's polite to ask, "Ist hier noch frei?" (Is this seat free?) before sitting down. Sharing a table is a great way to meet locals and enjoy the communal atmosphere.
- **Toasting:** When toasting with others, it's customary to make eye contact and say "Prost!" (Cheers!). Be sure to clink glasses gently, especially if you're using glass mugs, as this shows respect and care.

- **Cutlery Use:** In Germany, it's typical to keep your fork in your left hand and your knife in your right hand while eating. After finishing a meal, place your knife and fork parallel on the plate to indicate that you're done.

Tipping:

Tipping in Munich is appreciated but not obligatory. Here are some guidelines:

- **Restaurants:** Round up the bill or leave a tip of about 5-10% for good service. When paying, tell the server the total amount you'd like to pay, including the tip.
- **Cafes and Bars:** For smaller bills, it's common to round up or leave a small tip of €0.50 to €2.
- **Taxis:** It's customary to round up to the nearest euro or add a small tip of around 5%.
- **Hotels:** Tipping porters €1-€2 per bag and housekeeping staff €1-€2 per night is appreciated.

Festivals and Traditions

Munich is home to a variety of festivals and traditions, many of which offer a glimpse into Bavarian culture. Participating in these events can be a highlight of your visit, but it's important to observe local customs and etiquette.

Oktoberfest:

Oktoberfest is Munich's most famous festival, attracting millions of visitors each year. Here are some tips for enjoying the festival respectfully:

- **Traditional Attire:** Wearing traditional Bavarian attire, such as Lederhosen for men and Dirndls for women, is common at Oktoberfest. If you choose to wear these outfits, make sure they are worn respectfully and authentically.
- **Beer Tents:** Beer tents can get crowded, so be patient and polite when finding a seat. It's customary to toast with those around you, and sharing tables is the norm. Remember to pace yourself when drinking, and always drink responsibly.

Public Holidays and Religious Observances:
Munich observes several public holidays and religious traditions, which may affect the availability of services and the atmosphere in the city. For example:

- **Sunday Quiet:** Sundays in Munich are considered days of rest, and many shops and businesses are closed. It's a time for family, leisure, and religious observance, so expect a quieter atmosphere in the city.
- **Easter and Christmas:** During religious holidays like Easter and Christmas, many locals attend church services and observe family traditions. Be mindful of these customs, and if attending a religious service, dress modestly and observe the quiet reverence of the occasion.

Public Behavior and Environmental Awareness

Munich residents take pride in their city's cleanliness and orderliness. Respecting public spaces and being mindful of your environmental impact is important.

Public Behavior:
- **Quiet Hours:** Munich has designated quiet hours, typically from 10:00 PM to 6:00 AM, when loud noises and disturbances are discouraged. Be respectful of your neighbors and the local community by keeping noise levels down during these times.
- **Littering:** Littering is frowned upon in Munich, and the city provides plenty of public trash bins and recycling options. Always dispose of your trash properly and take care of public spaces.

Environmental Awareness:
- **Recycling:** Germany has a strong culture of recycling, and Munich is no exception. Separate your waste according to the bins provided, which are often color-coded for different materials (e.g., glass, plastic, paper).
- **Water Conservation:** Tap water in Munich is of high quality and safe to drink. It's also common practice to conserve water, so be mindful of your water usage, especially in hotels and public facilities.

Respecting Local Traditions

Munich has a deep cultural heritage, and respecting local traditions and customs is a way to show appreciation for the city's history and people.

Religious Respect:
- **Churches and Religious Sites:** Munich is home to many beautiful churches and religious sites, which are often open to visitors. When entering a church, dress modestly, speak quietly, and avoid taking flash photography during services. It's also customary to remove your hat as a sign of respect.
- **Public Holidays:** Many public holidays in Munich are based on religious traditions. On these days, it's common for shops to be closed and for locals to spend time with family. Be aware of these holidays and plan your activities accordingly.

Cultural Sensitivity:
Munich's residents take pride in their Bavarian heritage. Showing interest in and respect for local customs, such as traditional music, dance, and cuisine, is a great way to connect with the culture. Avoid making jokes or comments that could be perceived as disrespectful to Bavarian traditions or people.

E. Emergency Contacts and Useful Numbers

Emergency Numbers

In Germany, there are several universal emergency numbers that you can dial from any phone, whether it's a mobile or landline. These numbers are toll-free and available 24/7.

General Emergency (Police, Fire, Ambulance): 112

This is the primary emergency number in Germany for any life-threatening situation, including medical emergencies, fires, or needing police assistance. Operators can often speak English, so don't hesitate to call if you're in need of urgent help.

Police (Non-Emergency): 110

Dial this number if you need police assistance in a non-life-threatening situation, such as reporting a theft or a lost item. The police can also help direct you to other services if needed.

Medical Emergencies

If you experience a medical emergency or require urgent care, Munich has several hospitals with emergency rooms (Notaufnahme) that are equipped to handle a wide range of health issues. You can go directly to the nearest hospital or call 112 for an ambulance if you need immediate transportation.

Klinikum der Universität München (LMU) – Großhadern Campus
- **Address:** Marchioninistraße 15, 81377 Munich
- **Phone:** +49 89 440050

One of Munich's largest and most comprehensive hospitals, offering 24/7 emergency services.

Klinikum rechts der Isar – Technische Universität München
- **Address:** Ismaninger Str. 22, 81675 Munich
- **Phone:** +49 89 41400

Another major hospital in Munich, known for its excellent medical care and emergency services.

Poison Control Center: +49 89 19240

If you or someone you're with has ingested something potentially harmful, call this number for immediate advice on what to do. This service is available 24/7 and can provide information on poisoning and toxicology.

Pharmacies (Apotheken)

Pharmacies are widely available throughout Munich, and they can provide over-the-counter medications, as well as fulfill prescriptions. If you need medication outside of regular business hours, some pharmacies offer extended hours or 24/7 service.

- **Finding an Open Pharmacy:** If you need a pharmacy during the night or on Sundays, look for a "Notdienst" sign outside the pharmacy, which indicates that it's on duty for emergency services. You can also check online or ask at any pharmacy for the nearest one that's open.

- **Pharmacy Locator Website:** www.aponet.de (this site helps you find open pharmacies based on your location).

Lost or Stolen Items

If you lose your passport, wallet, or other important items, or if you believe they've been stolen, it's important to report the incident to the local authorities and your embassy as soon as possible.

Lost Property Office (Fundbüro):
- Address: Oetztaler Str. 19, 81373 Munich
- Phone: +49 89 23396010

Munich's central lost and found office where you can report lost items or check if something you lost has been turned in.

Reporting a Theft:
If you need to report a theft, go to the nearest police station or call the non-emergency police number, 110. It's important to obtain a police report, especially if you need to make an insurance claim or replace stolen travel documents.

Embassies and Consulates

If you're a foreign national and need assistance with passports, visas, or other consular services, you should contact your country's embassy or consulate in Munich. Here are a few key contacts:

U.S. Consulate General Munich
- Address: Königinstraße 5, 80539 Munich
- Phone: +49 89 28880
- Website: https://de.usembassy.gov/

UK Consulate General Munich
- Address: Möhlstraße 5, 81675 Munich
- Phone: +49 89 211090
- Website: https://www.gov.uk/world/germany

Canadian Consulate General Munich
- Address: Leopoldstraße 23, 80802 Munich
- Phone: +49 89 2199500
- Website: https://www.canada.ca/

Australian Consulate General Munich
- Address: Sendlinger-Tor-Platz 5, 80336 Munich
- Phone: +49 89 2424060

- Website:
  https://germany.embassy.gov.au/

Tourist Information and Support

Munich's tourist information centers are excellent resources if you need help with directions, bookings, or general advice during your stay.

Tourist Information Centers:
- **Marienplatz Center:** Located in the heart of Munich, this center offers maps, brochures, and advice in multiple languages.

Hauptbahnhof (Main Train Station) Center: Conveniently located for travelers arriving by train, this center provides information and support for your visit.

Munich Tourist Information Phone Number: +49 89 23396500
  Call this number for general tourist information, help with bookings, or to ask questions about navigating the city.

Transportation and Public Services

Understanding how to navigate the city's public transport and services is crucial, especially in case of an emergency.

MVV (Munich Public Transport) Customer Service: +49 89 41424344

For questions related to public transport routes, tickets, or lost items on the U-Bahn, S-Bahn, trams, or buses, contact MVV's customer service.

Taxi Services:
Munich Taxi Central: +49 89 21610

Taxis are widely available throughout the city. You can call the above number to request a taxi or find one at designated taxi ranks around the city.

Other Useful Numbers

Roadside Assistance (ADAC): +49 89 222222

If you experience car trouble or need roadside assistance, the ADAC (German Automobile Club) offers emergency services throughout Germany.

Munich Airport Information: +49 89 97500

For flight information, lost baggage, or other inquiries related to Munich Airport, this number connects you to the main information desk.

Water/Electricity Emergency Services:
- **Water Emergency:** +49 89 23612412
- **Electricity Emergency:** +49 89 23612509

These numbers are for emergencies related to water or electricity services within Munich.

Chapter 13: Munich for Families

A. Family-Friendly Attractions

1. Deutsches Museum – The German Museum

Overview:
The Deutsches Museum is one of the world's largest and most prestigious museums dedicated to science and technology. It's a must-visit for families, offering interactive exhibits and hands-on activities that engage children and adults alike. The museum's diverse collection spans topics from aerospace and transportation to physics and energy, making it a fascinating educational experience for all ages.

What to Expect:
- **Interactive Exhibits:** The museum's interactive exhibits are designed to make learning fun. Kids can explore a replica of a coal mine, pilot a plane in a flight simulator, or even conduct their own science experiments in the Children's Kingdom (Kinderreich), an area specifically designed for younger visitors.
- **Special Sections for Kids:** The museum has several sections tailored to children, including the "Kids' Kingdom," where young ones can play and learn through a variety of hands-on activities. There's also a dedicated area where children can learn

about natural phenomena in a playful environment.
- **Temporary Exhibitions:** The museum regularly hosts temporary exhibitions, which often include themes that appeal to children, such as space exploration, robotics, and marine life.

Contact and Information:
- **Location:** Museumsinsel 1, 80538 Munich
- **How to Get There:** The museum is easily accessible by public transport. The closest U-Bahn station is Isartor (U1, U2, U5, U8).
- **Opening Hours:** Daily from 9:00 AM to 5:00 PM.
- **Website:** www.deutsches-museum.de

2. Hellabrunn Zoo

Overview:
Hellabrunn Zoo, officially known as Tierpark Hellabrunn, is one of Munich's most beloved family attractions. Located in a beautiful natural setting along the Isar River, the zoo is home to over 750 species of animals from around the world. The zoo is designed to replicate the natural habitats of the animals, providing an immersive experience for visitors.

What to Expect:

- **Animal Encounters:** Hellabrunn Zoo offers plenty of opportunities for close-up animal encounters. Families can watch elephants, giraffes, and lions in spacious enclosures or visit the petting zoo where kids can interact with goats and other friendly animals.
- **The Polar World:** One of the highlights of the zoo is the Polar World exhibit, where visitors can see polar bears, penguins, and seals. The underwater viewing areas allow children to watch these animals swim and play in their naturalistic environments.
- **Play Areas and Picnic Spots:** The zoo also features several playgrounds and picnic areas, making it easy to take breaks and enjoy a meal surrounded by nature. The Adventure Playground is particularly popular with kids, offering plenty of space to run, climb, and explore.

Contact and Information:
- **Location:** Tierparkstraße 30, 81543 Munich
- **How to Get There:** The zoo is accessible by U-Bahn (U3 to Thalkirchen) or by bus (Lines 52, 135).
- **Opening Hours:** Daily from 9:00 AM to 5:00 PM (hours may vary by season).
- **Website:** www.hellabrunn.de

3. Nymphenburg Palace and Park

Overview:

Nymphenburg Palace, one of Europe's most beautiful baroque palaces, is a family-friendly destination that offers a blend of history, art, and outdoor fun. The palace and its expansive park provide plenty of activities to keep the whole family entertained, from exploring opulent rooms to boating on the palace's canals.

What to Expect:

- **Palace Tour:** Families can tour the palace's grand rooms, including the famous Hall of Mirrors and the beautiful frescoed ceilings. The palace also houses the Marstallmuseum, which displays historic carriages and sleighs used by Bavarian royalty.
- **The Park and Gardens:** The vast gardens surrounding Nymphenburg Palace are perfect for a family day out. Children will love running through the manicured lawns, exploring the hidden pathways, and discovering the various pavilions scattered throughout the park. The gardens are also home to the Nymphenburg Porcelain Manufactory, where you can see delicate porcelain pieces being crafted.
- **Boat Rides:** During the warmer months, families can rent paddle boats and row around the palace's canals, providing a unique perspective of the gardens and palace.

Contact and Information:

- **Location:** Schloss Nymphenburg 1, 80638 Munich
- **How to Get There:** The palace is accessible by tram (Lines 16, 17) or by bus (Lines 51, 151).
- **Opening Hours:** The palace is open daily from 9:00 AM to 6:00 PM (April to October) and 10:00 AM to 4:00 PM (November to March). The park is open year-round.
- **Website:** www.schloss-nymphenburg.de

4. BMW Museum and BMW Welt

Overview:
For families with an interest in cars and technology, the BMW Museum and BMW Welt are must-visit attractions in Munich. Located next to the BMW headquarters, these venues offer an exciting look into the history and future of automotive innovation.

What to Expect:
- **BMW Museum:** The BMW Museum takes visitors on a journey through the history of the BMW brand, showcasing classic cars, motorcycles, and engines. The exhibits are interactive, with plenty of hands-on activities and multimedia displays that make the museum engaging for children and adults alike.

- **BMW Welt:** BMW Welt is a modern exhibition space where visitors can explore the latest BMW models, including cars and motorcycles. Families can sit inside the vehicles, learn about cutting-edge technology, and even take a test drive if they meet the requirements. The futuristic architecture of BMW Welt is also a highlight, providing a dynamic and visually stunning experience.
- **Kids' Programs:** The BMW Museum and BMW Welt offer special programs and workshops for children, where they can learn about engineering, design, and technology through fun, hands-on activities.

Contact and Information:

- **Location:** Am Olympiapark 1, 80809 Munich
- **How to Get There:** The museum and BMW Welt are easily accessible by U-Bahn (U3 to Olympiazentrum).
- **Opening Hours:** The BMW Museum is open Tuesday to Sunday from 10:00 AM to 6:00 PM. BMW Welt is open daily from 9:00 AM to 6:00 PM.
- **Website:** www.bmw-welt.com

5. Sea Life Munich

Overview:

Located in the heart of the Olympiapark, Sea Life Munich is an aquarium that offers a fascinating glimpse into the underwater world. With a wide range of marine life on display, this family-friendly attraction is both educational and entertaining.

What to Expect:

- **Marine Exhibits:** Sea Life Munich features over 30 tanks and displays, housing more than 4,000 sea creatures from various habitats. Kids can marvel at sharks, rays, sea turtles, and colorful tropical fish as they explore the different sections of the aquarium.
- **Interactive Experiences:** The aquarium offers several interactive experiences, such as touch pools where children can gently touch starfish and sea anemones. There are also daily feeding sessions and talks where visitors can learn more about marine conservation.
- **Ocean Tunnel:** One of the highlights of Sea Life Munich is the ocean tunnel, where visitors can walk through a glass tunnel surrounded by water, offering a 360-degree view of sharks, rays, and other sea creatures swimming above and around them.

Contact and Information:

- **Location:** Willi-Daume-Platz 1, 80809 Munich

- **How to Get There:** Sea Life Munich is located in the Olympiapark, accessible by U-Bahn (U3 to Olympiazentrum).
- **Opening Hours:** Daily from 10:00 AM to 5:00 PM (hours may vary by season).
- **Website:** www.visitsealife.com

B. Parks and Playgrounds

1. English Garden (Englischer Garten)

Overview:
The English Garden is one of the largest urban parks in the world, even bigger than New York's Central Park. It's a favorite among locals and tourists alike, offering a vast expanse of greenery, winding paths, and numerous attractions that cater to visitors of all ages. It's the perfect place for families to spend a day outdoors, with plenty of space for kids to play and adults to relax.

What to Expect:
- **Play Areas:** The English Garden has several playgrounds spread throughout the park, each with swings, slides, and climbing structures suitable for children of different ages. The playgrounds are well-maintained and often shaded, making them a comfortable spot for kids to burn off some energy.

- **Family Activities:** Families can rent paddleboats on the Kleinhesseloher See, a picturesque lake in the heart of the park, or simply enjoy a leisurely walk or bike ride along the park's many trails. The park is also home to the Japanese Tea House, where families can participate in traditional tea ceremonies.
- **Picnic Spots:** The English Garden is full of idyllic picnic spots. Bring a blanket, pack a lunch, and enjoy a meal surrounded by nature. For a true Bavarian experience, visit one of the park's beer gardens, like the one at the Chinese Tower, where parents can enjoy a cold beer while kids play nearby.

Contact and Information:

- **Location:** The English Garden stretches from the city center to the northeastern edge of Munich. Main entrances are near Odeonsplatz and Universität.
- **How to Get There:** Accessible by U-Bahn (U3, U6 to Universität) or tram (Lines 16, 18 to Tivolistraße).
- **Opening Hours:** Open year-round, 24 hours a day.
- **Website:** www.muenchen.de (for general park information)

2. Westpark

Overview:

Westpark is a large public park located in the western part of Munich. It's known for its beautiful landscaping, cultural gardens, and numerous recreational facilities. The park offers a variety of activities and attractions that make it a great destination for families looking to spend time outdoors.

What to Expect:
- **Playgrounds:** Westpark features several playgrounds, each with unique themes and play equipment. The playgrounds cater to children of different ages, with areas designed for toddlers as well as older kids. The sand playground near the Rosengarten is particularly popular, with plenty of space for digging and building.
- **Cultural Gardens:** Westpark is home to several themed gardens, including a Chinese garden, a Japanese garden, and a Thai sala. These gardens are peaceful spots where families can learn about different cultures and enjoy the tranquil surroundings.
- **Family-Friendly Activities:** The park has a large lake with paddleboats available for rent, a mini-golf course, and several open spaces for playing ball games or flying kites. During the summer, the park also hosts outdoor cinema events, where families can watch movies under the stars.

Contact and Information:

- **Location:** Westpark is located in the Sendling-Westpark district of Munich.
- **How to Get There:** Accessible by U-Bahn (U6 to Westpark) or bus (Lines 54, 130).
- **Opening Hours:** Open year-round, 24 hours a day.
- **Website:** www.muenchen.de

3. Olympiapark

Overview:
Built for the 1972 Summer Olympics, Olympiapark is a sprawling complex that remains one of Munich's most popular recreational areas. It's not only a place for sports and events but also a fantastic destination for family outings, with various attractions and activities that appeal to all ages.

What to Expect:
- **Adventure Playground:** Olympiapark is home to one of Munich's most exciting adventure playgrounds, featuring climbing structures, slides, and a large sandbox. The playground is designed to encourage imaginative play and physical activity, making it a hit with energetic kids.
- **Olympic Tower and Roof Climb:** Families with older children may enjoy taking a trip to the top of the Olympic Tower, where you can get panoramic views of the city. For a more adventurous experience, consider the

roof climb tour, which takes you on a guided walk across the roof of the Olympic Stadium.

- **Green Spaces and Lakes:** The park's vast green spaces are perfect for picnics, sports, or simply relaxing in the sun. There are also several lakes where you can rent paddleboats or take a leisurely stroll along the water's edge.

Contact and Information:

- **Location:** Olympiapark is located in the northern part of Munich.
- **How to Get There:** Accessible by U-Bahn (U3 to Olympiazentrum).
- **Opening Hours:** Open year-round, 24 hours a day.
- **Website:** www.olympiapark.de

4. Hirschgarten

Overview:

Hirschgarten, known as "Deer Garden," is a large park located in the western part of Munich. It's famous for its beer garden, the largest in Munich, but it's also a wonderful place for families, with plenty of space for children to play and explore.

What to Expect:

- **Deer Enclosure:** One of the park's unique features is the deer enclosure, where families can observe deer in a natural setting. The enclosure is a big hit with kids, who enjoy watching and sometimes feeding the deer.

- **Playground and Open Spaces:** Hirschgarten has a large playground with swings, slides, and climbing frames. The park also offers vast open spaces where children can run freely, play ball games, or enjoy a family picnic.
- **Beer Garden:** While the adults enjoy a refreshing drink at the beer garden, children can play safely within view, making it an ideal spot for a relaxed family outing.

Contact and Information:
- **Location:** Hirschgarten is located in the Neuhausen-Nymphenburg district.
- **How to Get There:** Accessible by S-Bahn (S1, S2, S3, S4, S6 to Hirschgarten).
- **Opening Hours:** Open year-round, 24 hours a day.
- **Website:** www.hirschgarten.de

5. Botanischer Garten München-Nymphenburg (Botanical Garden)

Overview:
The Botanical Garden in Munich-Nymphenburg is a beautiful and educational destination for families. Covering 21 hectares, the garden is home to over

14,000 species of plants, as well as a range of themed gardens, greenhouses, and water features. It's a peaceful spot where families can enjoy nature, learn about plants, and take a break from the hustle and bustle of the city.

What to Expect:
- **Greenhouses:** The garden's greenhouses are a highlight, featuring exotic plants from around the world. Children will be fascinated by the variety of tropical plants, cacti, and orchids, as well as the small ponds filled with koi fish.
- **Themed Gardens:** The outdoor gardens are divided into different themes, such as the rose garden, alpine garden, and medicinal plant garden. Each section offers something unique to explore and learn about.
- **Educational Programs:** The Botanical Garden offers educational programs and workshops for children, where they can learn about botany, ecology, and conservation in a fun and interactive way.

Contact and Information:
- **Location:** Menzinger Str. 65, 80638 Munich
- **How to Get There:** Accessible by tram (Line 17 to Botanischer Garten).
- **Opening Hours:** Daily from 9:00 AM to 6:00 PM (hours may vary by season).
- **Website:** www.botmuc.de

C. Child-Friendly Dining Options

1. Hofbräukeller

Overview:
Hofbräukeller is a traditional Bavarian beer hall and beer garden located in the Haidhausen district, not far from the city center. It's a popular spot with locals and tourists alike, known for its lively atmosphere, hearty Bavarian food, and spacious beer garden. What makes Hofbräukeller especially great for families is its large outdoor playground, which keeps kids entertained while parents enjoy their meal.

What to Expect:
- **Playground:** The beer garden at Hofbräukeller features a well-equipped playground where kids can climb, slide, and swing to their heart's content. The play area is within easy view of the outdoor seating, allowing parents to relax while keeping an eye on their children.
- **Kid-Friendly Menu:** The restaurant offers a dedicated children's menu with popular options like schnitzel, sausages, and pasta. Portions are generous, and the menu includes fun, kid-friendly presentations.
- **Bavarian Specialties:** For the adults, Hofbräukeller serves classic Bavarian dishes such as roast pork with dumplings, Weisswurst (white sausage), and pretzels, all

of which can be enjoyed with a cold beer from the Hofbräu brewery.

Contact and Information:
- **Location:** Innere Wiener Str. 19, 81667 Munich
- **How to Get There:** Accessible by U-Bahn (U4, U5 to Max-Weber-Platz) or tram (Lines 15, 25).
- **Opening Hours:** Daily from 11:00 AM to midnight.
- **Website:** www.hofbraeukeller.de

2. Augustiner-Keller

Overview:
Augustiner-Keller is one of Munich's oldest and most beloved beer gardens, offering a family-friendly environment where both kids and adults can enjoy Bavarian hospitality. Located near the Hauptbahnhof (main train station), it's a convenient and welcoming spot for families looking to experience traditional Munich dining in a relaxed setting.

What to Expect:
- **Family-Friendly Atmosphere:** The beer garden at Augustiner-Keller is spacious and shaded by chestnut trees, creating a pleasant environment for families. The outdoor area

is ideal for kids to explore and play, while parents enjoy a leisurely meal.

- **Children's Menu:** The restaurant offers a children's menu featuring simple, tasty dishes like chicken nuggets, fries, and pasta. The portions are tailored to younger appetites, and the menu includes drinks and desserts that kids will love.
- **Traditional Bavarian Cuisine:** The main menu includes a wide variety of Bavarian favorites, such as roast chicken, sausages, and potato salad. The relaxed setting and friendly service make it easy for families to enjoy a traditional meal together.

Contact and Information:
- **Location:** Arnulfstr. 52, 80335 Munich
- **How to Get There:** Accessible by S-Bahn (all lines to Hackerbrücke) or tram (Lines 16, 17).
- **Opening Hours:** Daily from 10:00 AM to midnight.
- **Website:** www.augustinerkeller.de

3. Café Glockenspiel

Overview:
Café Glockenspiel is a charming café located in the heart of Munich, right on Marienplatz. Known for its stunning views of the Glockenspiel and its cozy, welcoming atmosphere, this café is a great choice

for families looking for a relaxed meal or snack while exploring the city center.

What to Expect:
- **Kid-Friendly Options:** Café Glockenspiel offers a wide range of options that kids will enjoy, including pancakes, waffles, and sandwiches. The breakfast menu is particularly popular, with a variety of sweet and savory dishes that appeal to both children and adults.
- **Family-Friendly Atmosphere:** The café's central location and relaxed vibe make it a convenient stop for families. Large windows offer a fantastic view of the Glockenspiel, which is sure to captivate children during the hourly chimes and figurine performances.
- **High Chairs and Facilities:** Café Glockenspiel provides high chairs for younger children and has facilities to accommodate families, making it a hassle-free option for a meal with kids.

Contact and Information:
- **Location:** Marienplatz 28, 80331 Munich
- **How to Get There:** Accessible by U-Bahn and S-Bahn (all lines to Marienplatz).
- **Opening Hours:** Daily from 9:00 AM to midnight.
- **Website:** www.cafe-glockenspiel.de

4. Vapiano

Overview:
Vapiano is a popular family-friendly restaurant chain that specializes in Italian cuisine. Located throughout Munich, Vapiano offers a casual dining experience with fresh, made-to-order pasta, pizza, and salads. It's a great option for families looking for a quick and satisfying meal in a relaxed setting.

What to Expect:
- **Customizable Meals:** At Vapiano, meals are made to order, allowing you to customize dishes to suit your children's tastes. Kids can watch as their pasta or pizza is prepared right in front of them, which adds a fun, interactive element to the dining experience.
- **Children's Menu:** Vapiano offers a dedicated children's menu with smaller portions of pasta, pizza, and desserts. The menu also includes drinks and kid-friendly snacks.
- **Casual Atmosphere:** The restaurant's casual, self-service setup makes it easy for families to dine at their own pace. There's no need to wait for a server, which is particularly convenient for families with young children.

Contact and Information:

- **Location:** Various locations in Munich, including one near Stachus (Karlsplatz).
- **How to Get There:** Accessible by U-Bahn and S-Bahn (all lines to Karlsplatz/Stachus).
- **Opening Hours:** Typically from 11:00 AM to midnight (hours may vary by location).
- **Website:** www.vapiano.com

5. Hans im Glück

Overview:
Hans im Glück is a modern burger restaurant that offers a wide variety of gourmet burgers in a family-friendly environment. With multiple locations in Munich, this trendy spot is known for its creative menu, fresh ingredients, and unique decor inspired by the fairytale of the same name.

What to Expect:
- **Kid-Friendly Menu:** Hans im Glück's menu includes options that appeal to children, such as classic cheeseburgers, chicken burgers, and fries. The burgers are customizable, allowing you to adjust toppings and sauces to suit your child's preferences.
- **Vegetarian and Vegan Options:** The restaurant also offers a range of vegetarian and vegan burgers, making it a great choice for families with diverse dietary needs.

- **Relaxed Dining:** The restaurant's casual and cozy atmosphere makes it easy for families to enjoy a meal together. The whimsical decor, featuring birch trees and natural elements, creates a fun and inviting setting for both kids and adults.

Contact and Information:
- **Location:** Various locations in Munich, including near Sendlinger Tor.
- **How to Get There:** Accessible by U-Bahn (U1, U2, U3, U6 to Sendlinger Tor).
- **Opening Hours:** Daily from 11:00 AM to midnight (hours may vary by location).
- **Website:** www.hansimglueck-burgergrill.de

D. Tips for Traveling with Kids in Munich

1. Plan Your Itinerary with Breaks

When exploring a city as rich in history and culture as Munich, it's easy to pack your schedule with back-to-back activities. However, children, especially younger ones, can become tired or overwhelmed if there's too much to do in one day. To avoid burnout, plan your itinerary with regular breaks.

Tips:

- **Include Downtime:** After visiting a museum or historical site, plan for some downtime in a park or a café where kids can relax and recharge. Parks like the English Garden or Westpark are ideal for this.
- **Mix Indoor and Outdoor Activities:** Balance the day with a mix of indoor attractions (like museums) and outdoor spaces (like playgrounds or gardens) to keep things varied and interesting for children.
- **Don't Overpack Your Day:** Allow plenty of time between activities, so you're not rushing from one place to the next. This relaxed pace will make the day more enjoyable for everyone.

2. Use Public Transport Wisely

Munich has an excellent public transport system, which makes getting around the city with kids convenient and straightforward. The U-Bahn (subway), S-Bahn (commuter train), trams, and buses are all reliable and safe options for families.

Tips:
- **Stroller-Friendly Transport:** Most of Munich's public transport is stroller-friendly, with designated areas for prams and easy access to platforms via elevators or ramps. However, some older tram or bus models might be a bit more challenging, so plan accordingly.

- **Day Passes:** Consider purchasing a day pass (Tageskarte) for unlimited travel on all public transport within the city. This is more economical if you plan to use public transport multiple times throughout the day.
- **Peak Hours:** Try to avoid traveling during peak hours (7:00-9:00 AM and 4:00-6:00 PM) when public transport can be crowded, making it more difficult to navigate with children.

3. Pack Essentials for a Day Out

When spending the day exploring Munich, it's important to pack the essentials to ensure your family is comfortable and ready for anything the day might bring.

Tips:
- **Snacks and Water:** Always carry snacks and water, especially if you're visiting attractions where food might not be readily available. Munich has many small bakeries and shops where you can pick up fresh pretzels, fruits, and other treats.
- **Weather-Appropriate Clothing:** Munich's weather can be unpredictable, so bring layers and a small umbrella or rain jacket. In summer, don't forget sunscreen and hats for sun protection.
- **Entertainment:** Bring a small toy, book, or tablet to keep children entertained during

longer stretches of travel or while waiting at restaurants.

4. Choose Child-Friendly Accommodation

Selecting the right accommodation can make a big difference when traveling with kids. Look for places that offer family rooms, extra amenities for children, and a convenient location.

Tips:
- **Family Rooms:** Many hotels in Munich offer family rooms or suites with extra beds or cribs. Some also provide amenities like bottle warmers, high chairs, and children's toiletries upon request.
- **Location:** Choose accommodation that's close to major attractions or public transport hubs to minimize the need for long commutes. Staying near a park or playground can also be beneficial for quick outdoor breaks.
- **Breakfast Included:** Hotels that offer breakfast included can simplify your morning routine and ensure everyone starts the day with a full stomach.

5. Take Advantage of Family Discounts

Many of Munich's attractions offer discounts or special rates for families, which can help make your trip more affordable.

Tips:

- **Family Tickets:** Look for family tickets at museums, zoos, and other attractions. These tickets often provide a discounted rate for two adults and one or more children.
- **Free Admission for Young Children:** Some attractions offer free admission for children under a certain age (usually 5 or 6 years old). Always check the admission policy before purchasing tickets.
- **Discount Cards:** Consider purchasing a Munich City Pass or other tourist discount cards that offer reduced admission to multiple attractions, as well as free public transport.

6. Be Mindful of Local Customs

Munich is a city with deep-rooted traditions and a strong sense of community. Teaching your children about local customs can enhance their cultural experience and help them feel more connected to the places they visit.

Tips:

- **Quiet Time:** Munich residents value peace and quiet, especially during certain times of the day, such as Sunday mornings. Encourage your children to speak softly and respect the tranquil atmosphere in places like churches or public transport.
- **Public Behavior:** In public places, especially in more formal settings like

restaurants or museums, it's important to keep noise levels down and encourage polite behavior.

- **Learn a Few German Phrases:** Teaching your children basic German phrases like "Guten Tag" (Good day), "Bitte" (Please), and "Danke" (Thank you) can be a fun way to engage with the local culture and make a positive impression.

7. Safety First

While Munich is generally very safe, it's still important to take basic precautions to ensure your children's safety during your travels.

Tips:

- **Stay Together:** Munich's streets and attractions can be busy, so make sure to stay close to your children, especially in crowded areas.
- **Emergency Contact Info:** Write down your hotel's address and phone number, and give it to older children in case they get separated. It's also a good idea to teach your children how to identify police officers or security staff if they need help.
- **Know the Emergency Number:** The emergency number in Germany is 112. Make sure older children know this number and how to use it if necessary.

8. Explore Child-Friendly Attractions

Munich offers a wealth of attractions that are particularly enjoyable for children. Make sure to include a mix of educational and fun activities in your itinerary.

Tips:
- **Interactive Museums:** Visit museums like the Deutsches Museum or the BMW Museum, which have interactive exhibits designed to engage young minds.
- **Outdoor Adventures:** Spend time in parks like the English Garden or Olympiapark, where kids can run, play, and explore in a safe, natural environment.
- **Animal Encounters:** Don't miss the Hellabrunn Zoo, where children can see animals up close and enjoy playgrounds and picnic areas.

Conclusion

We're delighted you chose the Munich Travel Guide 2024 as your companion for exploring Bavaria's captivating capital. It's been an honor sharing Munich's gems with you, and we hope this guide has enriched your visit, whether it's your first or you're a returning enthusiast.

We've strived to provide a comprehensive picture of Munich, highlighting its iconic landmarks like the Marienplatz and the Frauenkirche, its world-renowned beer gardens, and its vibrant cultural scene. We've also included practical information to ensure your trip is smooth and enjoyable.

Hopefully, our descriptions of Munich's attractions have inspired you to experience its unique blend of tradition and modernity. Whether you're here for Oktoberfest, to explore its artistic heritage, or to simply savor the Bavarian ambiance, Munich offers something truly special.

For history buffs, we've shared the stories behind Munich's rise as a cultural powerhouse, its architectural marvels, and its role in shaping European history. Understanding these facets will deepen your appreciation of the city.

We've also included practical tips, from navigating the city to dining recommendations, to ensure your experience is stress-free. The sections on family-friendly activities, local festivals, and day trips will help you make the most of your time here.

As your Munich adventure winds down, take a moment to reflect on the experiences and memories you've created. Munich is more than just a destination; it's a vibrant city brimming with history, culture, and warmth. We hope your time here has been as fulfilling and inspiring as it has been for countless others.

Thank you for choosing the *Munich Travel Guide 2024*. We hope it's been a valuable companion on your journey. May your travels continue to be filled with joy and discovery.

We wish you safe travels and many more adventures ahead. May you continue to find beauty in every corner of the world. Until next time, happy travels, and may your path always lead to wonderful experiences.

Servus und auf Wiedersehen!

The Munich Travel Guide 2024 Team

A Heartfelt Note to Our Readers

Greetings from Munich!

We're thrilled you chose our Munich Travel Guide 2024 to accompany you on your Bavarian adventure. We sincerely hope it's been a helpful companion, guiding you to the heart of Munich's magic.

We'd be incredibly grateful if you'd share your thoughts on the guide. Your honest feedback helps fellow travelers discover the best of Munich and motivates us to create even more enriching travel resources.

Thank you for your support, and we wish you many more unforgettable journeys ahead.

With warm wishes from Munich,

The Munich Travel Guide Team

Exclusive Bonus: Authentic Traditional Munich Recipes

As a special bonus for choosing the Munich Travel Guide 2024, we've included a selection of authentic traditional Munich recipes and preparation instructions. These dishes will allow you to bring the flavors of Bavaria into your home and relive the tastes of this beautiful city long after your trip. Here are some of the Munich recipes you should try:

1. Schweinsbraten (Roast Pork)

Ingredients:
- 3-4 lbs boneless pork shoulder or butt
- 1 tbsp caraway seeds
- 1 tsp salt
- 1/2 tsp black pepper
- 1 onion, sliced
- 2 carrots, sliced
- 2 cups dark beer
- 1 cup beef broth

Instructions:
1. Preheat oven to 350°F (175°C).
2. Score the pork skin and season with caraway seeds, salt, and pepper.
3. Sear the pork in a hot pan until golden brown on all sides.
4. Place the pork in a roasting pan, add the vegetables, beer, and broth.
5. Roast for 2-3 hours, or until the internal temperature reaches 145°F (63°C).

6. Remove the pork and let it rest. Strain the pan juices and thicken them for gravy.

7. Serve the Schweinsbraten with dumplings and sauerkraut.

2. Weißwurst (Bavarian Veal Sausage)

Ingredients:
- 1 lb ground veal
- 1/2 lb ground pork back fat
- 1/2 cup ice water
- 1 tsp salt
- 1/2 tsp white pepper
- 1/4 tsp ground nutmeg
- 1/4 tsp ground ginger
- 1 tbsp chopped fresh parsley
- Sausage casings

Instructions:

1. Combine all ingredients except casings in a bowl and mix well.

2. Stuff the mixture into sausage casings.

3. Poach the sausages in simmering water for 10-15 minutes.

4. Serve with sweet mustard and pretzels.

3. Obatzda (Bavarian Cheese Spread)

Ingredients:
- 4 oz Camembert cheese, softened
- 4 oz cream cheese, softened
- 1 tbsp butter, softened
- 1 small onion, finely chopped

- 1 tsp paprika
- 1/2 tsp caraway seeds
- Salt and pepper to taste

Instructions:

1. Mash all ingredients together until smooth and creamy.
2. Serve with pretzels or bread.

4. Apfelstrudel (Apple Strudel)

Ingredients:

- 1 package phyllo dough, thawed
- 1/2 cup melted butter
- 3-4 apples, peeled, cored, and sliced
- 1/2 cup sugar
- 1/4 cup raisins
- 1/4 cup breadcrumbs
- 1 tsp cinnamon
- 1/4 cup chopped walnuts (optional)

Instructions:

1. Preheat oven to 375°F (190°C).
2. Lay out phyllo sheets on a clean cloth, brushing each with melted butter.
3. Combine apples, sugar, raisins, breadcrumbs, cinnamon, and walnuts (if using).
4. Spread the filling over the phyllo, leaving a border.
5. Roll up the strudel tightly and brush with butter.
6. Bake for 30-40 minutes, or until golden brown.
7. Serve warm with vanilla sauce or ice cream.

5. Dampfnudeln (Bavarian Sweet Dumplings)

Ingredients:
- 2 cups all-purpose flour
- 1/2 cup warm milk
- 1/4 cup sugar
- 1 packet active dry yeast
- 1 egg
- 1/4 cup melted butter
- 1/4 tsp salt
- 1/2 cup butter
- 1/2 cup milk
- 1/4 cup sugar
- Vanilla sauce (optional)

Instructions:
1. In a bowl, combine warm milk, sugar, and yeast. Let stand for 10 minutes.
2. Add flour, egg, melted butter, and salt to the yeast mixture. Knead until smooth.
3. Cover and let rise in a warm place for 1 hour.
4. Divide the dough into 12 pieces and shape into balls.
5. In a large pan, melt butter with milk and sugar.
6. Place the dumplings in the pan, cover, and cook over medium heat for 15-20 minutes.
7. Serve warm with vanilla sauce (optional).

Made in the USA
Las Vegas, NV
01 December 2024

13142095R00205